TAROT

A Journey to Higher Consciousness

Cindy Zweibel

TAROT: A Journey to Higher Consciousness
Copyright © 2012 by Cindy Zweibel

Cover Illustration and Design by Cindy Zweibel

Cards from the Universal Tarot by Roberto de Angelis
Copyright © 2000 by Lo Scarabeo, used for this book,
were reprinted with permission from Lo Scarabeo

For contacting the author:
email address: czpent @aol.com

ISBN-13: 978 - 1470013615
ISBN-10: 1470013614

DEDICATION

This book is lovingly dedicated to Joy Srour,
my much beloved meditation and spiritual
development teacher, who made her
transition to the Other Side on
December 25, 2007.

She made a huge difference in my life
........and continues to lovingly teach me,
and guide my evolution in the journey

and

To God, The Creator, for giving me my life here
to experience the journey with,
making it possible for me to write this book,
that I hope with all my heart
will make a difference in touching the hearts
and lives of those who read it.

Tarot Prayer
To be read before studying this book

Ruler of the Universe, Power of Powers, Creator of all that is and Source of My Being, please open my mind, my heart and my senses to the wisdom of the Tarot with spiritual vision and spiritual hearing. Allow me the experience of having your wisdom come through my thoughts and words in working with the tarot.

Awaken my mind and fill my vessel with your light, that I may be a clear channel to receive the consciousness of each card and your intention for each card in it's application, not only for myself, but for all those I come into contact with who seek my counsel with it's wisdom.

Give me the ability to clearly receive your wisdom and light in my study and use of the tarot and let the force of your light shine through me in the unfolding of this process, that I may be a source of peace, love and light in this world.

Table of Contents

Acknowledgements

To my much beloved meditation and spiritual development teacher, Joy Srour, for the love and loving counsel she passed on to me. Joy made her transition to the other side on December 25, 2007, where she continues to lovingly teach me and guide my evolution in the journey. She made a huge difference in my life at all levels, including getting this book written, and I will love her for all eternity.

To Michael Santimauro for helping and supporting me at so many levels, that made this book possible.

To The Metaphysical Center of New Jersey for sponsoring me as their Tarot instructor since 1986.

To every student I have ever taught Tarot to in the past, present and future. They have inspired me to share what I am passionate about and have given me the incentive to be the best teacher I can be .

To the millions of clients I have read over the years who have allowed me to counsel them with the Tarot since 1973, and in the years to come. It's from studying the tarot patterns of their lives in their readings, as well as my own, that I continue my lifelong study of the tarot's application in life.

To Janet Berres for her delightful words of encouragement in getting this book out and for introducing me to Lo Scarabeo and Riccardo Minetti.

To Riccardo Minetti for his encouraging words, belief in my book, and getting me permission from Lo Scarabeo to use their tarot deck illustrations for this book.

To Lo Sacarabeo (a great company) for allowing me permission to use their Universal Tarot Deck illustrations for this book.

To God, for bringing all these people and experiences into my life.

My Story

My Story

It was early evening in the month of January 1982 when my life was forever changed. I had been praying to God for answers from the Source about life, and boy did I ever receive the answer to my prayer in the most unexpected and startling way! I was lifted out of my body into another dimension and this dazzling white light in a field of mist, unlike anything I had ever encountered or been prepared for before, entered my bedroom and spoke to me with a very physical voice. God was talking to me! No matter which room I went into God followed me, all the while instructing me about the power and value of thought.

Equally remarkable was the fact that my television was turned on by this force and videos were appearing on the screen in 3D, showing me possible future outcomes in the world that could be caused into being by freewill thought choices, positive or negative, made not only by me but by humanity. With this I was told to block out negative thoughts, to avoid unwanted outcomes.

The lessons given to me made everything I had learned about the Tarot, and years later, Kabbalah, (which as you will see later on in the book, the tarot is based on), come to life with a reality I could no longer doubt, however the actual learning of how to use the information became an ongoing life process of unfolding. In this book I will pass on to you my own experienced personal and professional life journey with each card and what I learned, with the help of my spirit guides along the way.

During that same evening I saw a multitude of red pyramids in the sky, followed by this huge green force field of light coming diagonally down into the soccer field, across the street from our home in Glen Rock, New Jersey. I would later learn that those red pyramids and the neon green force field I saw were UFOs, that to the normal eye would be invisible, but because I was in the astral realm, out of my body, my eyes were able to witness them undisguised. Approximately two years later, while in a bookstore, looking for explanations for the experiences I had gone through back in 1982, two books came tumbling down from the upper shelves, hitting my head and definitely getting my attention. Ironically enough and certainly no mere coincidence, they were the answers I was looking for. One was called "The Science of Thought Vibrations", which pretty much summarized the lessons I had learned from the Voice of God that evening back in '82. The other book was called "Secret Places of the Lion", whose cover showed a red pyramid, a green force field of light and a UFO, similar to what I had seen in the sky. It was so wonderful to have a picture to validate what I had seen!

My introduction to the tarot came in a most unusual way, and surely planned out by my spirit guides (more on that later). My older brother was in love with James Bond movies and I mostly got to go to those movies with him as a side benefit, but it was in one of the those movies, back in 1973, that I was introduced to the tarot. It was in "Live and Let Die" that I saw Jane Seymour playing the role of a high priestess reading tarot cards. While watching the movie, in somewhat of a surreal fashion, I saw my own face superimposed on the screen and felt as if it were me, not her, reading the cards. After that movie I got my first tarot deck and book and I was hooked!

I was amazed by how a little deck of 78 cards could know so much about someone and be so accurate about things that hadn't even come to pass yet. Little did I know when I first embarked on my study of the tarot, back in 1973, that this was no ordinary deck of cards. The tarot, I discovered, was an unbound book of the soul's journey through life, told through the universal and archetypal language of symbolism, and an ancient spiritual system, believed to be a pictorial form of the Kabbalistic Tree of Life.

With my earlier interest in dream interpretation, the movies, and using spiritual symbolism in my artwork, the tarot was a perfect evolution in my soul's direction in life. My life became a mirrored extension of my work and vice versa. I was learning about life through the tarot and learning about the tarot through life.

I used to beat around the bush telling people what I did for a living, because I didn't want to be judged by religious fanatics or be made to feel bad about myself by others, for not having a career that fit into mainstream society's expectations of what was considered the norm. I loved my work, considered it a job from Heaven, (which it actually really is) and I didn't want to subject myself to others, not yet ready to see another way of living, which will soon be known to all in the coming world shift of consciousness.

As soon as I committed myself to doing this work, doors in every arena of my life started to swing wide open, with my tarot work being the venue in which they all opened. This was a sign I was on the right track for me, regardless of what others thought.

The more I worked with the tarot the more it's mysteries unfolded. I noticed a lot of similarity between dreams, movies and tarot, in the creation of reality. I was fascinated by the way tarot mirrored how life functioned on a larger scale and I became aware that as a conscious observer you get to be an audience to the life movie of your own story. You are constantly creating, editing and recreating your story through the filter of the thoughts you are sending and receiving from the universe.

You are picking up other's energy all the time, just as a reader picks up energy from individual tarot cards. Your mind is receiving millions of impressions and doing mini readings every day of your life, whether you are conscious of it or not.

One of the biggest lessons I observed not only in tarot but in life as well, is that what you don't learn repeats itself and usually gets bigger and bigger, till you are forced to pay attention to it to avoid further pain. The lessons get harder as they go along, so the sooner you learn the lessons that come your way the easier it will be on you and your life. The scenes and situations may vary and the cast of characters may change, but the lessons and the relationships unhealed will remain the same.

The fact that this sort of knowledge could be revealed in a tarot card reading before it showed up in life proved to be the most valuable thing I learned a tarot card reading offered, not only for myself but for my clients as well. It was this observation that made me want to share what I had learned about the tarot with anyone and everyone, especially those ready and seeking such knowledge. I saw the immense value this tool could be to teach others how to master their state of consciousness and therefore their life as well.

Everything is a cell of a smaller and larger body, including all of us and our planet. All of our energies as a human species, come together to form group energies and we are all affected by each other's energies. What we learn or don't learn and experience individually or collectively affects our own lives personally and the world globally. What we heal in ourselves will also help in healing our world as well. We are all part of One Source energy we know as God, our Creator.

It is with great love that I share my passionate love of the tarot with all of you. I sincerely hope with all my heart, that the knowledge I share with you in these pages will enhance bringing peace and love into your life, and that you will use it to do the same for others, to enhance bringing peace and love in our world.

Introduction

Introduction

If there was a book out in the marketplace about your life, informing you of all the potential obstacles, rewards and events you could experience in it, most of you would purchase it in a minute, before it went out of print. If it were in a different language you'd either be eager to learn that language or find an interpreter who understands the language to read the book for you.

The tarot is such a book and the language that it speaks to us in is the universal language of symbolism, just like our dreams speak to us in symbols. **It is an unbound book of the story of the soul's journey through life** and it personalizes it's story to each individual who consults it's wisdom.

Whether we are aware of it or not, we read the language of symbolism everyday. We know to stop at a red light, go at a green light and that a yellow light means to slow down. We know that an icon inside a circle with a diagonal line through it means not to do something, and a multitude of other symbols we take for granted every day, including the very alphabet of our language, and in modern technology the icons on our computers.

The symbolism used in the tarot is archetypal and each card depicts a state of consciousness. When the cards are shuffled and laid out in a pattern known as a spread, they create a virtual roadmap of what an individual's consciousness is creating and reflecting back to them in the way of life experiences.

Life provides **a constant flow of information to the observer** whose awareness is tuned into it's many symbolic messages. Messages come in many forms - **coincidences, synchronicities,** a song playing on the radio in a store or location you happen to be in, that at that moment holds a special meaning or message for you, and many other **unending forms of**

transmission to the keen and **conscious observer.** It could be in a call coming in from someone you were just thinking about a few days or moments ago or something someone said to you in a single moment wherever you are, that is absolutely perfectly timed to just what you need to hear for inspiration - a new idea or some brilliant revelation that comes to you in **"Divine Timing"** in that **amazing experience of "Now".**

These are the ways **messages are transmitted to us. Nothing happens at random in life and no card appears or is chosen at random** when using the tarot. Everyone, every place and everything generates an energy force that transmits energy to another person, place or thing according to it's **intention.**

We as human beings are born into a physical body created by the sexual union of our parent's bodies, but our **"True Essence"** and **"Being"** is actually created of and by the **Spirit, Energy and Light of God - "The Source". Our True Being is Found Within. This Still Small Voice, found within us,** is the best way of tapping into the wise communication of **Source Energy.**

Through meditation our consciousness is elevated. The tarot at it's best, is an open eyed meditation. As human beings we are given the physical vehicle of a body to create in the **"World of Form", "The Material World"** as a **"Spark of Light Energy"** and **"Divine Child Of Our Creator" to Co-Create with Our Creator. We do this through our thoughts.**

Being spiritual energy in a physical body, we have the amazing ability to change the psychic energy we generate and transmit to others by the thoughts we think. **We attract the people and experiences we have in life because our thought energy is vibrating to the same frequency as their energy. This is what is known as "The Law Of Attraction".** The same holds true with the tarot. We attract the cards in a tarot card reading by the thoughts we are generating at the time of the reading. **The state of mind you're in at the time of a reading, be it positive or negative, will reflect the outcome shown in your cards,** just as it will in your life in that moment of time.

The tarot is an ancient spiritual, philosophical and psychological system believed to be a pictorial form of the Kabbalistic Tree Of Life, portrayed through the universal language of symbolism in a deck of 78 cards.

<u>The Tarot can be interpreted on 3 levels:</u>

Spiritual/Soul Lessons: <u>Consciousness</u>.
Psychological/Self-awareness: <u>Counsel</u>
Mundane/Prediction: <u>The Key Words</u>

22 of these cards, known as the Major Arcana, are believed to be an unbound book of the story of the Soul's journey through life, each card representing a spiritual lesson the soul must learn to gain Higher Consciousness. The remaining **56 cards known as the Minor Arcana, show us the processes we go through in our everyday living, that present us with the opportunity to learn these spiritual lessons and raise our level of consciousness.** These lessons when learned, give us a more joyful experience of life, **the Ultimate Goal Being to Return to Our "God Self", the Divine State of Love.**

It is important to know when you're embarking on a study of learning to read the tarot, either for yourself or for others, to **be patient with yourself and the process. You need to realize that it takes time to develop that psychic muscle of yours that has been lying dormant all these years.** Like anything else it requires practice. You have to learn to walk before you can run. I would highly recommend spending about 10 or 15 minutes a day with your cards in the beginning. Maintain a relaxed attitude and don't attempt to overdo it and learn everything in one day. You don't want to tire yourself out and lose interest before you really get started. **It takes time to develop the instinct of trusting the messages that you will receive from meditating on the cards,** and practice to get the inspiration they bring. **The more you use and study the tarot, the deeper and clearer your insights will be.**

The tarot is a remarkable tool that can provide you with astounding spiritual guidance. It will give you insights and answers to everyday happenings, that will amaze and entertain you time and time again for a lifetime, when used with the proper attitude, reverence and belief. If you **approach them with sincere desire, the cards will reflect that sincerity in their accuracy.** When **approached with an attitude of ridicule and mockery,** by either yourself or the one you're reading, **the cards will reflect that as well by giving inaccurate information.**

The Tree of Life, Tarot and Climbing Up the Ladder of Spiritual Evolution

The Tree Of Life

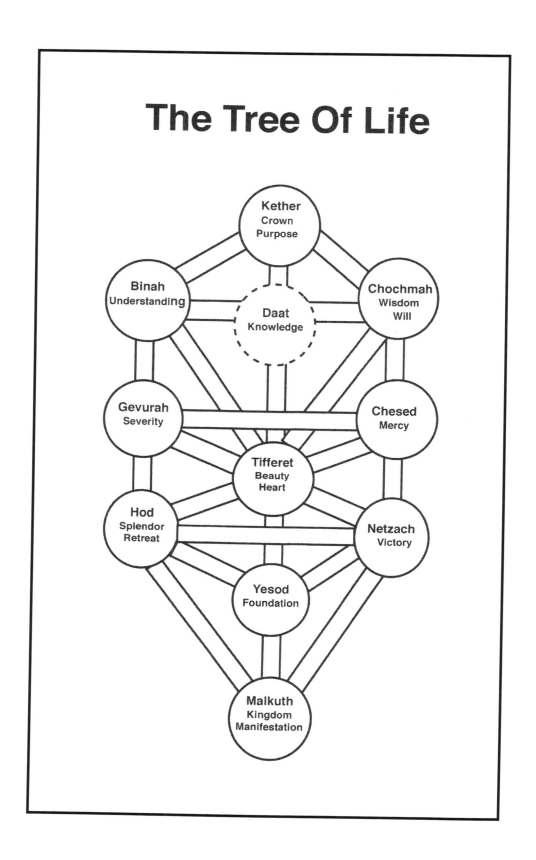

Tarot / Tree Of Life

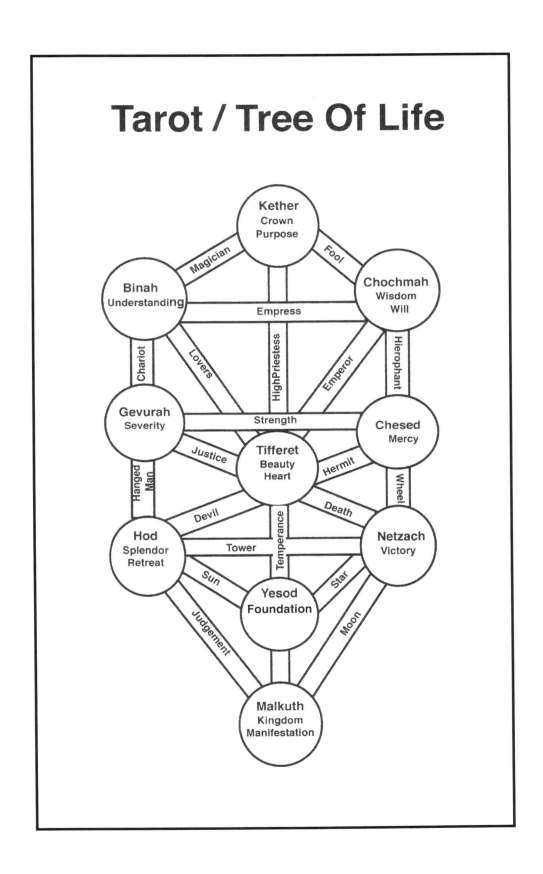

The Tree Of Life, Tarot and Climbing up the Ladder of Spiritual Evolution

The Tarot embodies within it the higher consciousness of the Kabbalah and it's Tree Of Life. This wisdom, when studied and practiced with concentrated focus, enables the soul to evolve up the spiritual ladder. **Each one of the Major Arcana cards corresponds to a path on the tree. The Tree of Life is a blueprint for creation.** There are many books that elaborate on this subject, that you can refer to. My purpose here is just to spark your interest, by bringing this awareness to your attention for further study and future reference sake. In this book you will acquire much of the the wisdom of the Kabbalah, but from the language and perspective of the Tarot.

By becoming a conscious observer of the symbols and patterns in a series of Tarot card readings over a period of time, you will learn how to be a reader of your Real World Life (the reality you are currently creating in the world of form with your thoughts) and vice versa. Tarot is in essence a symbolic mirror of your Real World Life. And to tell you the truth, neither one of them is actually real. They are both smaller and larger projections of your imagination - dreams in the form of lessons you have created. **Schoolhouse Earth is providing you with a playing field to grow the seed of your soul. "As above so below".**

The Real World and Tarot, technically speaking, both serve the same function. One is the life you are symbolically projecting from your thoughts (before it happens) onto the little movie in your tarot card spreads, and the other is the big movie of the life you have already manifested, currently projecting onto the world screen. Your thoughts form manifestations onto the material plane. Nothing happens at random. You are the creator of whatever is showing up.

Learn Tarot in 6 Easy Lessons:

(a.k.a. How to use this book)

"Tarot Class"
Lesson 1

Welcome to the classroom. Have a seat. Make yourself at home. I will be teaching you here as closely as I would be teaching you in person, in an actual classroom with me. Energetically I will be with you as you learn.

While learning the tarot can seem somewhat overwhelming and somewhat of a heavy subject to tackle at first, it is my deepest, heart felt desire to make it as light -filled and joyous a ride as I possibly can, which it should be, because once you get the hang of it that's precisely what it will be. **Using the key words I give you will get you reading immediately, so you can start having fun with it and feel encouraged right away. The deeper meanings, however, come later on and require practice.**

In a mirror of a mirror, microcosm of a macrocosm kind of parallel world, Tarot is somewhat like your Real World experience. It is the cosmic journey of your life while here at Earth School. Your true home is in the celestial realms, otherwise known as "The Other Side". Much like our grade schools and colleges here, you actually do get graded and have a report card here at Earth School that goes back home with you. This report card however, determines whether or not you get to ascend to higher planes in the spiritual realms. And that's what your here for - to grow your soul........and hopefully to have some fun in creating while you're doing it.

The first thing you want to do is pick out a tarot deck that you are drawn to that has pictures on all the cards. Not all decks are created equal. Many of them have the minor cards in geometric symbols, which is not suitable for a beginner just starting out, nor is it desirable even for more experienced readers. It requires a knowledge and an intuitive use of numerology and the symbology of the suits. For beginners I recommend using a deck that is illustrated with the symbols instructed by Arthur Waite. The deck I am using to illustrate this book is a fine choice. It is The Universal Tarot, published by Lo Scarabeo.

Next thing you will want to get is a wooden box to put your cards in and a silk, cotton or natural fibered piece of fabric to wrap them in, before storing them in the box. This keeps the energies contained on the cards intact, while still allowing them to breathe. The cards and the reading of them is all about energy and the sensing of those energies, which we will get into a little later on. See the section **Tarot Supplies I Recommend.**

The next things you will need are a solid colored cloth (or felt) to lay the cards on while you are reading them, and a felt tip pen to write and trace the cards on your cloth with, using The Celtic Block Layout Tracing map I have provided for you in the Spreads chapter of this book. This cloth will be your " Tarot Cheat Sheet" Cloth. For the cloth, I recommend felt for starting out because it doesn't require sewing the edges to prevent any fraying. It is easy to trace on with your felt tip pen, which you will be doing later on. I will instruct you how to do that when we start working on tarot spreads. Tarot spreads are the names given to cards laid out in a specific manner and pattern that enable a reading to be rendered.

You will need to have a ballpoint pen on hand to write the card key words onto each card. Either that or copy, cut and paste them onto your cards. You will find them on your Card Key Cheat Sheets listed in the Table of Contents. This will get you up and running much quicker as a reader and help you build trust in developing your intuition, from not having to memorize the cards right away. I also suggest getting a composition notebook and pen you like to write with for journaling, which is optional but highly recommended. It will help you to get the most out of your tarot card reading journey's experiences. What this does is make you your first client to practice on.....and who better to practice on then the one person you know will be available for you to read whenever you darn well please 24/7.

What I suggest is this.......As you learn the cards and spreads: Pick a card or do a layout for each day, depending on where you are in your learning curve, then date it and write what you believe it is telling you on the facing page of your journal. Then observe the next day what actually occurred, to see how accurate you were, and write down and date any new observations you learned about. Take notes of any new meanings that may come to you. Create a section in your journal to jot down meanings that come to you personally, that differ from the meanings given in this book.

These meanings will be your own guide's methods of communicating messages for you personally.

Learning how to meditate will increase your reading ability, however even just working with the tarot on a regular basis will be training your mind to focus and concentrate. The cards themselves are an open eyed meditation.

Next I want you to read the sections: **History, Introduction, The Science of Thought Vibrations, The Law of Attraction, Energy Pictures, and The Tree of Life,** so you will understand where Tarot comes from, and a bit more on how and why it works. This will help you become a more informed and better reader.

You have just completed lesson 1. Well done. You can now go on to lesson 2.

"Tarot Class"
Lesson 2

Welcome to our second class. In this class I want you to read the section on **The Major Arcana and Reversals. The Major Arcana tells the story of the soul's journey through life. In a reading it will show you what spiritual lessons you need to learn.** Copy the key words in the white border of the Major Arcana cards. This will help you get quickly used to their meanings.

Imagine you're in an actual classroom with me and other students studying with you. You look around the class and you kinda get a vibe about how each person feels to you. Then a person walks through the door with an angry disposition. You're already starting to formulate a sense of how you feel about this person's energy. It probably doesn't "feel" too good. Then a person walks through the door with a very happy disposition. You're starting to formulate a sense of how you "feel" about this person's energy. It probably " feels" good to you.

Start to notice how you "feel" with different people, whether it's while you're on the phone or in person with them. Look at each major card, one at a time, and start to sense how you "feel" when you look at it, just like you did with your imaginary classmates. Do the same thing with the people in your life. Later on you will be doing this with your clients or people you read for. Doing this will begin to train you how to sense energy.

You may also wish to check the section **Symbols, Signs and Colors** now for further info to help you. Your own impressions however are the best, just as in dream interpretation.

Personally, I find it's better to use your own imagination and visual impressions. Ask yourself what the pictures look like to you, for each card you are looking at. What you see may be something altogether different then the meaning of the cards. Jot these impressions down or store them in your memory. Your spirit guides may work better with these impressions, in giving you messages, because of how you relate to them. Let me give you an example: Many years ago one of my students thought the nine of cups looked like teeth and gums, so whenever she saw this card in a reading (depending on where it showed up in a spread) she would interpret it as a need for dental work.

Read and try doing **The Question and Answer Spread** with just the Major Arcana cards. By beginning to do even a simple spread like this right away, you will feel encouraged by your early accomplishment, and the excitement of being able to read answers to your questions so soon into your study. Before you do this, however, imagine a circle of white light around you for energy protection.

Another thing you may want to do is fan out the major cards and just pick one card for the day. The meaning of this card is similar to getting a message in a fortune cookie. You can do this for each day. Jot down in your journal what card it is, the date and the meaning. When the next day comes, see how it fits with what actually happens. By our 6th class you can do this with larger spreads. It is important to focus on your question and what you want to know while shuffling and cutting the cards, because you are putting the energy of the question into the deck. You can shuffle whatever way you wish. When through shuffling, cut the deck into three piles and then join all three piles back into one pile again, whichever way you want. Proceed with the spread after shuffling.

You have just completed lesson 2. Well done. You can now go on to lesson 3.

"Tarot Class"
Lesson 3

Welcome to our third class. In this class I want you to **read the first half of the section on The Minor Arcana.** Study **The Cups and The Wands.** Go over each card and get impressions of what the pictures look like to you. Record anything that comes to mind and date it in your journal. You want to do this with each card in the deck. Write the key words in the white border of each card. By not having to put so much emphasis on remembering the meanings, your mind can then relax, which makes more room for your intuition to get activated. Intuition gets you better messages. But of course this takes time and practice.

Wands represent ideas, projects or jobs and Cups represent emotions, values and relationships. The court cards usually represent people, and 2 or more in the same suit generally represent a couple or family members. Sometimes they will show a mature younger person or immature older one. The suit of a court card may indicate one of the zodiac signs it's represented by or a certain hair color of a person. Sometimes the suit indicates a personality type or how you will know them. For example: Wands may be someone from work or cups may be someone in your personal life. The suits also represent the seasons. When uncertain which meaning to go with, mention all the above as possibilities, saying it could be one or the other or all of these. Don't be afraid of making mistakes. Practice makes perfect. Read the section on **Yes and No Spreads** and try doing that now. **Just read the aces at this stage.** Later on you can read the other cards in this spread for further info.

You have just completed lesson 3. Well done. You can now go on to lesson 4.

"Tarot Class"
Lesson 4

Welcome to our fourth class. In this class I want you **to read the the second half of the section on The Minor Arcana**. Study **The Swords and The Pentacles.** As you did in our last class, go over each card and get impressions of what the pictures look like to you and record anything that comes to mind and date it in your journal. Write the key words for the Swords and Pentacles in the white border of each card.

The Swords show you how you deal with the problems, conflicts and challenges in your life and the Pentacles show how you deal with the financial and career aspects of your life. The Swords court cards may be people you are struggling with or those who have difficult personalities. The Pentacles court cards may be people whose focal point is "green"... as in money or globally related issues. Sometimes the court suits deal with the hair color or zodiac sign associated with it, as we learned in the last class. And again...when you're not certain, mention several possibilities.

Try doing the spreads we did in the last two classes, only this time use the whole deck, and read the additional cards you didn't read before, now that you have all the meanings. Remember, it is important to focus on your question while shuffling, cutting and picking the cards. Use your left hand to pick cards. The reason for this is because the left hand is closer to the heart.

Observe the suits that are next to one another. For example swords cards next to pentacles could indicate money problems, lack consciousness or overcoming these issues.

You have just completed lesson 4. Well done. You can now go on to lesson 5.

"Tarot Class"
Lesson 5

Welcome to our fifth class. **In this class we are now ready to do our first full spread.** Before we start I want you to get out your felt (or fabric), your felt tip pen and the blank or advertising card in your tarot card deck, and **trace each card listed on The Celtic Block Spread Sheet onto your felt. Next write what is on the Cheat Sheet Map onto your felt.** This will be what you use to do your readings on. **Because the instructions and meanings of each card location are right in front of you, you will be able to do a reading right away,** if you have already copied the key meanings on each card, as I suggested in the previous classes. If you haven't done that, use your Key Words Cheat Sheet to refer to. One other thing I want you to know before you attempt the Celtic Block Spread is that **once you have the cards down in the order of the spread, read the cards by where your eyes are drawn first. Numerical order no longer needs to be applied**, unless you choose to see it that way.

At this junction I would normally do sample readings with members of the class, in order to demonstrate how to do a reading, but for our purposes here, **go to The Sample Reading section in the book and study it up to the portion of The Celtic Block.** If you are adventurous you can include the portion with The Higher and Lower Pyramid. **This is your demonstration reading.** Next I want you to try reading the cards for yourself, following the instructions, or find a friend or family member to do a reading for. If you are reading yourself, record the reading to listen back later on, or jot down what you read in your journal and date it. If you are reading a friend or family member tell them you are a student and ask them to give you feedback afterwards or during the reading to know if you are on track.

Don't be afraid to make mistakes. You might just be right and if you don't say it you will never know. If the person you're reading can't relate, try again to get a different message from what you see. The more you try it the easier it will get and in time your intuition will increase and make your readings more interesting and accurate. **Sometimes you may be picking up messages accurately, but the client may not be open or ready to hear the information at the time of the reading.** When this happens, listen to your intuition and stay with your gut feelings.

In order to get a feeling for putting a story together, I want you to imagine yourself outdoors in an imaginary setting, like a strip mall. Picture a traffic light with two cars that have hit one another trying to get in front of each other. There is a police car and people surrounding the accident. There is broken glass on the lot and slight damage to one of the cars. By viewing the accident, you are looking at all the elements and probably putting a story together in your mind about what might have potentially happened. You do the same thing **in doing a tarot card reading. You look at all the elements - what cards are next to others, their location and how they relate to each other to put a story together**.

The Tarot, like life, is based on relationships- everything and everyone is in relationship to everything and everyone. This also includes timing. In the case of a tarot card reading, sequence would take the place of timing and the cards would represent people, places and things.

The Aces and Major Arcana cards, representing zodiac signs, give you clues of monthly and seasonal timing. When two cards representing zodiac signs, sharing a mutual month, show up next to each other I generally suspect the mutual month as a clue for timing. Otherwise the two months of a zodiac sign, in just a single card, could be a timing clue. It all depends where the cards land, just as in our imaginary strip mall scene.

Circle yourself with light (in your imagination) for energy protection, and ask your spirit guides to help you with wisdom and counsel, whenever you start doing a reading.

Learn how to meditate. I can't emphasize this enough. One basic method I can teach you, that I cover in my real classroom is as follows:

HOW TO MEDITATE

Sit with your spine upright on a chair, with your feet uncrossed and flat on the ground. Lay your hands on your lap, uncrossed and palms upright, thumbs touching your index finger. Gently close your eyes. Shake out any tension from the day. Mentally tell each part of your body to relax, from head to toe. Take three deep breaths (from your stomach area). Next picture an opening at the top of your head and imagine a white light streaming down into your body, flowing down your arms into your hands, and down your legs to your feet. Imagine a pillar of light above you, going through you and down into the center of the earth. Go into the silence for 10 - 20 minutes. Then gently begin to feel yourself coming back into your body and slowly open your eyes and come back to the room.

Ideally you want to do a 20 minute meditation every day, preferably at the same time each day and before you begin doing readings for the day.

You have just completed lesson 5. Well done. You can now go on to lesson 6, our final class.

"Tarot Class"
Lesson 6

Welcome to our sixth and final class. By this class my students are generally up and running doing readings for themselves and others, and hopefully in this classroom in a book environment you are doing the same.

If you haven't already read the portion of the sample reading with the higher and lower pyramid, go ahead and do so now. Then give it a try. Readings can be done for people over the phone or for those not present by shuffling and cutting the cards while focusing on the person's name that you want to read. Call someone you know and ask them if they'd like to get a reading. Let them know you're a tarot student so they will be willing to give you feedback. You read the cards just as if they were there but talk it into the phone.

Practice doing the readings you have learned for yourself and others over and over till it becomes more comfortable, and allow yourself to try new ways of seeing the cards to receive messages. Continue to meditate, as this will facilitate better readings. Also remember as I told you in the last class, before doing a reading silently ask your guides to provide you with wisdom and counsel for the one you are reading and that it be for their highest good. You'll be amazed at how this can really make a difference in your readings.

Best wishes in your journey with the Tarot. Thank you for allowing me to guide you as your Tarot Teacher in this classroom environment. I wish I could have met you all personally, but in energy we have already made a connection by your reading this book. Energetically I will continue to support you as grow with the tarot.

You have just completed lesson 6. Well done. Congratulations ! You made it.

Tarot Supplies I Recommend

Use a silk cloth or scarf to wrap cards in and a wooden box to store them in. Silk velvet pouches are also a nice touch as an alternative. Lo Scarabeo's Universal Deck, the one I have used in this book, is a good deck to work with. Get a composition book and pen to keep a Tarot Journal - get feed back from your own readings on what works for you, with recorded and dated readings for yourself.

History

History

The actual origin of the tarot remains somewhat obscure, however many attempts have been made to unveil its true ancestry. Many of these theories began with the dissection of the word **TAROT** itself:

<u>According to the Egyptians</u> the word **Tarot** means the **Royal Road** or **Royal Path** which stems from the word **Tar**, meaning **Road** and **Ro**, which means **King** or **Royal**.

<u>The Hindu word</u> for **Cards** is **Taru** and the Sanskrit word, **Rota** (which is an anagram of the word tarot), means **Wheel**, as in **Wheel Of Life**.

<u>The Hebrew word</u> **Torah**, which means **Divine Law** and represents the **first five books of the Old Testament**, is another possible derivative.

<u>The Chinese word</u> **Tau** and the Arabic word **Tariqa** are also clues, as both of these words mean **The Way**.

The most recurring theory on the origin of the tarot is that it came from the hieroglyphics that appeared on the chamber walls leading from the sphinx to the pyramids in ancient Egypt. It was in these underground locations that secret societies and mystery schools formed and instructed their initiates in the ancient wisdom believed to have been passed down from Atlantis. The symbolism of these hieroglyphics, which then became the tarot, denoted initiation phases and lessons of self development, which were used to raise an individual's level of consciousness.

The neophytes of these societies had to go through these lessons, followed by testing periods to prove their worthiness, in becoming adepts of The Brotherhood, or Great White Brotherhood, as they were commonly known.

The Science of Thought Vibrations

The Science of Thought Vibrations

The tarot is a marvelous tool for personal growth, self awareness and psychic development. It can symbolically mirror what thought patterns are preventing you from moving forward and living in the now, that when cleared, will free up your passion and bliss, revealing the true God Force within you, your Higher Self, allowing you to experience more love in your life.

The first and foremost thing to know, before we tackle such a topic, is that **each and every one of us is a Co-Creator with God, the Source and Creator of our Being and it's through our thoughts that we Co-Create. We are all cells in One Infinite Body of Intelligence and Light, existing in an Ocean of Energy. Each and every one of us is actually no more separate from one another than our pinky finger is separate from our hands, so each of our lives is affected by each other's life. The only thing that appears to separate us is the physical body we clothe ourselves in, in this material world of form.**

Now that may seem a little hard to understand, but think back to when you were in grade school. Remember when one person did something wrong and the whole class had to stay after school as a result? And now on a larger scale think about politics. We are all affected by each other's votes as to who becomes our next president. And on a larger scale when our president makes a decision about national and international affairs like war and ways to fight or flight from pollution of our environment, we are all collectively affected and responsible, because each and every one of our votes or lack of votes put that president in office to represent us. And so on and so on down the line to larger and larger and smaller and smaller scales of examples, till you realize that it all starts with you, the individual. It's kind of like the husband who comes home from a lousy day at work and yells at his wife, the wife gets all upset and yells at the kids, and the kids go out and kick the cat.

The point I'm trying to illustrate here is that each of our individual lives are very, very important and the best way to help yourself, your family, your country, your world and your universe is to work on yourself first, because that's where it all begins. **How you live your life affects not only your life but a whole chain of lives around you. Thought energy in motion has a rippling effect like a stone or pebble being thrown into a pond. We live in an ocean of energy that is constantly being directed and channeled through our thoughts.** In order to work on yourself you need to become consciously aware of your thoughts, because it's through your thoughts that **you create your own reality and it's totally up to you whether you create a heaven or hell** out of your life.

It's here that the tarot becomes such a wonderful teaching tool, because the tarot mirrors what is going on in the subconscious mind and makes it visible. This is much like how all the people and events in our lives mirror such information on a larger scale. **With the tarot we can see a miniature movie of our life before our eyes, before it happens in physical form.** We get to witness, in preview, how our thoughts have created our past, present and future to come, should our thoughts continue as is at the time of a tarot card reading. After a while you begin to notice certain patterns and when this occurs you start to recognize that it's not the people and events in your life that are causing what's happening, it's your attitude, outlook and perception in handling them, causing whatever is presented to you. You begin to see that **everything happens for a reason.**

Just as in life, the tarot will teach you that **every experience you generate you've attracted to yourself to learn some particular lesson. Generally, the lesson is to seek out the thoughts in your subconscious mind that you may not be aware of, that need to be corrected and updated in the now, to help you live more effectively in the present.** Old negative tape thoughts from your past, still living in your subconscious mind's impressions, create havoc with your life in it's present form, the current now. We have all been gifted with free will and learning how to properly use our free will is no different than learning that right thinking produces harmony in your life and wrong thinking produces pain and suffering. You may not always have a choice as to the circumstances in your life, but you will always have a choice as to how you're going to react versus not react, by just observing and dealing with things as lessons to be learned.

You see **your mind is like a garden and your thoughts are like seeds. When you plant positive, loving, harmonious seeds in your garden that's what you can rightfully expect to grow around you. If you're careless and you don't weed out the negative, hateful, worry seeds from growing, you can also expect your garden to produce these effects in your experiences, that are not so harmonious.** When you don't weed out the negative thoughts you will know it. They will keep creeping back into your thought patterns till the forces around you force you to pay attention to them. You may notice yourself banging into little things at first and then slightly bigger things start to happen, like falling down. If you still don't listen the lessons get bigger and harder to get your attention. Something like a car accident or an illness could come next. Even where you get hit or what type of illness you take on will indicate where you need to change your thoughts. Therefore when big or little unpleasant things start happening to you, look inside yourself to what thoughts you need to release and let go of, to avoid such experiences again.

The reason this happens is really no different from the way that everything else in life operates. It's all very scientific. **Everything in life vibrates and it's the rate of vibration that distinguishes one person or thing from another. It is because of this that we are attracted to certain kinds of music, other people, other things and events.** All matter is composed of energy, and energy is composed of vibrating atoms which combine and form molecules. **We are energy.** When you have a thought it creates what is known as a thought form and this thought form, carrying a vibration all it's own, starts an energy in motion. This energy then, with all its vibrating atoms, seeks other atoms that have a similar vibratory rate to form molecules and it is the way these molecules combine that matter manifests.

Loving thoughts have a very high vibratory rate while thoughts of evil have a very low vibration. When you think loving thoughts you attract loving patterns occurring into your life and when your thoughts are evil this likewise is what you attract to yourself. The same holds true

for positive and negative thoughts. Think positive thoughts of health, happiness and material abundance and this is what pattern you bring into your life. Think negative thoughts of fear, worry, hate and anger and you attract patterns in your life that are in harmony with these vibrations. This is known as **the Universal Law of Attraction, "Like Energy Attracts Like Energy".**

It's because the tarot mirrors what is going on in the subconscious mind, through the symbols on the cards, that a reading can be rendered on an individual before things have actually manifested. This then provides the opportunity to make changes while the energy is still just in the subconscious. With such information being brought to the conscious mind, the individual is then provided with the opportunity to make the necessary changes in their thoughts, before they have the chance to form into materialized matter. **If you dissect the word information you get - "in form" -ation. That says it all right there. We learn and gain wisdom from what we cause into form.**

Use the tarot to teach yourself how to meditate on life. It will give you a more personal connection to the reality you create in your everyday life. **It is by this process of awakening and raising our level of consciousness that we restore our power from within. This is where the still small voice of our Divine Self, our individual portion of the God Force and Spark of Creation resides.**

Because we are all cells of an even larger body, the earth, the earth being a cell of an even larger body, the universe, and the universe being a cell in the body of God, our gift of free will has made us all powerful creators for better or for worse, both individually and collectively. Use your thoughts and the tarot wisely. It can be a powerful tool for healing at many levels.

Energy Pictures

The following pictures were taken with high speed cameras specializing in showing the energy field around a person. **Energy expands, contracts and changes colors around the field of a person according to their thoughts.** This energy is also referred to as our aura.

I am showing you these pictures to make the idea more real to you that **our thoughts are energy fields, effecting other energy fields.** Everyone and everything has an energy field and each of us constantly effects other fields, positively and negatively, as well as personally and globally, whether we do it consciously or unconsciously. **We exchange energy, taking and giving, by who we spend time with and by the locations we are in. Locations and things are effected by the energies of many thinkers.** The more dominant the feeling behind the thought, the stronger the energy impression gets and effects other fields of energy.

These shots in particular were taken of myself at various times in past years, some just head shots, some just finger tips and some just showing the energy over the body in the areas of the chakras (spinning energy fields in our etheric body).

In pictures H-1 and H-2, I was about to go through a crisis and my energy field was heightened by the presence of one of my spirit guides, who actually showed up on the photo! (In picture H-2 he appears just above and around my head). We are never alone. **We all have spirit guides and teachers that are ever present by our side. They are especially there in our time of need.** In H-3, I was experiencing much passion and happiness. In H-4 past lives showed up. F-1 and 2 show before and after prayers were said. In C-1 you can see the chakras as well as the aura changing, from shots that were all taken at different times.

Headshot Energy Field-1
(H -1)

Headshot Energy Field -2
(H - 2)

Headshot Energy Field -3
(H - 3)

Headshot Energy Field -3
(H - 4)

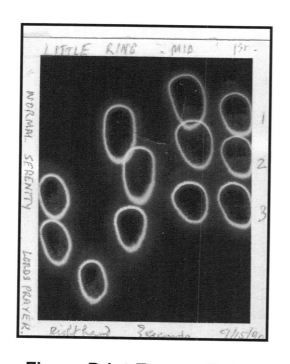

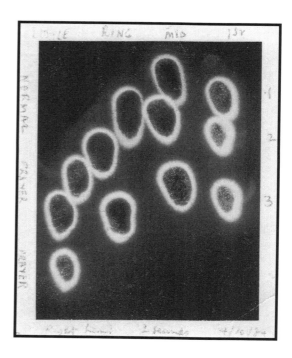

Finger Print Energy Field -1
(F - 1)

Finger Print Energy Field -2
(F - 2)

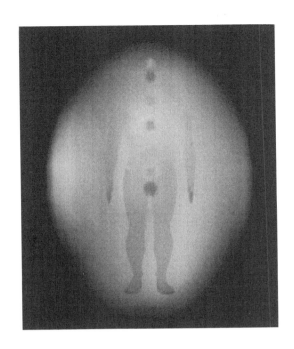 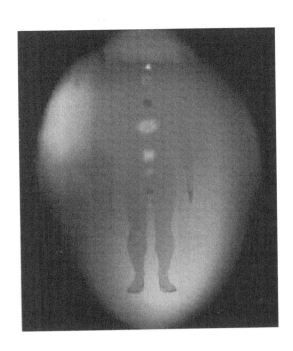

Chakras & Aura Energy Field-1
(C - 1)

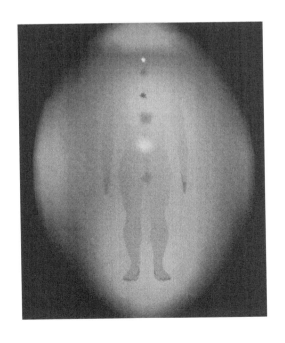 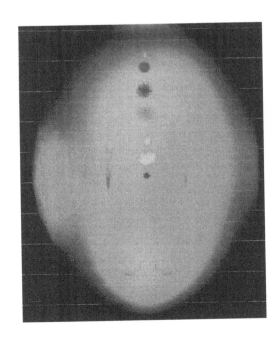

Reversals

Reversals

Here at Earth School there are polarities of opposites in everything - positive/negative, light/dark, good/bad, love/fear, male/female, big/small, microcosm/macrocosm, etc.. **My take on reversals is this:** Since we don't alter things to be upside down and right side up in the macrocosmic "Real World" we live in, to figure out whether things are positive or negative here, then we sure as heck don't need to have things be both upside down and right side up in the microcosmic world of Tarot we are using here, to figure out what the heck is going on in the Real World. Life is a journey of experiencing both the bad with the good on the road to perfecting our soul's development and gaining higher consciousness. The various relationships and many of the scenarios presented to you in this life were designed by you and your spirit guides before you were even born, according to the karmic soul lesson specifications you decided to take on in this round of incarnating, making corrections from previous lives. The reason you did this was to assist your soul in the process of climbing up the evolutionary ladder to better and more enjoyable places of existence in the celestial realms. That world is your true home. This physical world you are living in now is just a temporary dwelling place, a boarding school so to speak, you came to in order to facilitate the education of your soul. You knew you could get better living quarters back home by going another round here because the soul polishing equipment for evolving is much better here then there.

Each card in the tarot represents a level of consciousness represented in archetypal symbolism, that has both positive and negative traits. **Just like in real life, you must use your own "power of discernment," to determine whether what you are "looking" at with your eyes and "feeling" in "energy" with your body, is positive or negative.** The negative aspect of each card would be the opposite of it's positive interpretation. The cards next to one another and where they are placed in your spreads will give you clues as to whether to read them as positive or negative. Even if the card is seen as a negative you want to find the positive in it, just as in life. There is a lesson and gift of growth in every adversity, therefore, focus on the positive aspect in the negatives.

The Major Arcana

The Major Arcana

The Major Arcana is a symbolic form of The Tree of Life from the Kabbalah. Each one of it's cards is represented by one of the 22 letters of the Hebrew alphabet. **This portion of the Tarot deck tells the story of The Soul's Journey through the world**.

Each one of the 22 cards of the Major Arcana, numbered 0 to 21, has a vibrational significance of its own, representing a state of consciousness in symbols. Each card also has a successive and interactive relationship to each of the other cards. Cards representing zodiac signs can refer to people, timing or influence of that particular sign.

The cards can be read at many levels - Spiritually, by showing the lessons in consciousness the soul must learn, Psychologically by giving therapeutic counsel, and then there's the Mundane interpretation, where the cards are used for Prediction. The latter basically means that the cards can tell you what is most likely to occur in the person's future based on their past and present thoughts.

The Soul is represented by the The Fool card and the number zero. He has come from the world of Spirit and he's now entering the material world, unaware of his individual identity or why he is here. A lifetime of lessons lies ahead of him, hopefully well learned and leaving him a bit wiser by the time he goes back home.

His mission is to discover his purpose and further perfect his soul by acquiring wisdom through his creations. When he returns back home to the Spirit World he will be graded on what he accomplished here and by what he has learned.

Keywords
Uranus. Super Conscious Mind.
Collective Unconscious. Faith. Risk.
New Beginnings. Innocence. Naive

The Fool

Consciousness

The Fool represents the soul, who is embarking on a journey through life in the world. He also represents the Super Conscious Mind (the Collective Unconscious). Much like Dorothy in The Wizard of Oz, walking along the yellow brick road (the spiritual path) in the land of Oz, he too, is trying to find his way back home (while here on earth). You are a student of life (a spirit taking on a human form) walking along your own spiritual path in the world of material form, before you go back home (Heaven). He is the bohemian free spirit, the eternally youthful soul, full of hopes and dreams. Dancing to the tune of his own drum, he's bopping about with fresh new ideas and vitality, as he steps out into the world. He's the virtual embodiment of inspiration and spiritual love. He is way too trusting and isn't even thinking of the people behind him who may want to snag that bag he is carrying behind him. He is totally oblivious to the negative forces and predators out there who may see him as easy prey. Yet fresh down the chute into this world he's foreign to, he has no direction yet. He needs to learn to listen to his own inner voice, guidance from the Spirit World and then apply it to this world. Utilizing such support behind him, others taking advantage of him will suffer the consequences of their actions against him.

Counsel

The Fool needs to watch out for those meanies who want to rip away that light-filled, loving innocence of his, kill his spirit, and steal his ideas. They're jealous of that upbeat, happy-go-lucky soul of his because theirs has gotten tainted by the negative forces in this world. They want to bring him down with their negativity and corruptness. They're going to have a field day with with this guy, or so they think. He will eventually bounce right back, after he's healed his wounds and eventually see it as a learning experience. Spirit will hear his calls (prayers) and help him. He must live, learn and continue to follow his dreams in spite of all obstacles, because he is here to perfect his soul, making corrections along the way as part of the process.

IL MAGO
LE BATELEUR

I

THE MAGICIAN
EL MAGO

DER MAGIER

DE MAGIËR

Keywords
Mercury. Focus. Channeling. Leadership.
Concentration. As above so below.
Conscious mind. Graduation

The Magician

Consciousness

The Magician represents the Conscious Mind. He is master of the elements, indicated by the symbols of all four suits he has on his table. He has learned to focus his energies with concentrated intent, and channel the universal energies towards his desired goals. He demonstrates the Universal Law, "As above so below", bringing Heaven to Earth. The Magician reminds us of our inherent powers as Children of God (Gods In Training - G.I.T.s). Two thousand years ago Jesus, the Master of Masters, told the world to follow his example, telling us we too are Gods, capable of all he did and more. His message, that "We and the Father are One" and that with the faith of a single mustard seed (believing) we could move mountains, is just as true now as it was when he walked upon the planet. We too must learn to be the magicians we truly are and use the powers our Creator has given us wisely to represent him in the world, by bringing Heaven to Earth. Be the Love and Light that God is and you will find it.

Counsel

Whenever you see the Magician, he is telling you to use the power of intention to focus your energy with concentration. Believe in your ability to achieve whatever it is you so desire. He wants you to know that You and the Father are One and together all things are possible. Your greatest gift to The Creator, for the gift of your life here in the world, is to be of service to your fellow man. Use your Divine power wisely, direct your thoughts for the positive good of all and be an example for others to follow. Channel the Christ Consciousness, bringing Heaven to Earth, and be of service in the area of life that is of greatest interest to you. What you love doing is where you'll usually find your talent, purpose and mission.

Keywords

Moon. Subconscious Mind, ESP. Psychic.
Choice, Spiritual Wisdom. Mystery
School. Positive vs. Negative

The High Priestess

Consciousness

The High Priestess represents the Subconscious Mind. Somewhat like the moon she holds, she is a reflector of "The Light" (The wisdom of The Creator). She gets her wisdom from within. She is highly psychic, sensual and very tapped into the metaphysical aspects of life. She understands the hidden mysteries of creation and she's spiritual to the core. Behind that curtain lies the secrets of the universe. She has learned to use the negative dark moments in her life for positive enlightenment. She brings light to the world with her counsel of spiritual wisdom.

Counsel

Be cautious of negative thoughts rooting negative energy in the garden of your subconscious mind. Don't give them a chance to gestate and develop into larger negative reality creations. Don't put off today what will be larger and harder for you to get rid of later, requiring more of your precious life's energy and time to correct. Learn from the best teacher in the world - the one inside yourself, your Higher Self's divine wisdom. Take the time to know who you are from within. Awaken your own inherent psychic abilities or seek counsel from one who has, who can help you. Develop yourself spiritually. You are here in Earth School to learn from all your experiences - positive and negative. Learn to block out negative thinking and choose positive actions. Something you are seeking answers to may be hidden from view right now or going through a period of gestation and development.

L'IMPERATRICE
L'IMPERATRICE

III

THE EMPRESS
LA EMPERATRIZ

DIE HERRSCHERIN

DE KEIZERIN

Keywords
Venus. Abundance. Mother Figure.
Nurturer. Ideal Female For Male.
Unconditional Love. Compassion.
Prosperity Consciousness

The Empress

Consciousness

The Empress represents the positive, nurturing, unconditionally loving Mother aspect of The Creator. The first person in life we are influenced by is our mothers. Was your experience with your mother a positive one or negative one? Since not all mothers are the same, our experience with our mothers can greatly influence how unconditionally loving and nurturing we will be with ourselves and others in the world, later on in life. We all want positive, loving experiences in our lives, so we must ultimately learn to love ourselves if we are to attract love in the world. The archetypal mother figure is the one who will offer her children milk and cookies to comfort their pains and sorrows when they are having a bad day. In a world where money and material things provide us comfort and pleasure, The Empress also represents abundance in our lives. She can be our actual mother, a mother figure, or being the mother to ourselves or others. For a male, The Empress represents his ideal partner. By focusing on the positive thoughts, words and actions in ourselves and others, we attract and maintain this energy presence in our lives.

Counsel

Seeing The Empress in a reading is a reminder to be unconditionally loving to yourself and others, the way you would like a mother figure to be to you. She is telling you to appreciate yourself - your flaws, your talents, and your history, as the mother aspect of The Creator would. No one can do the job for you. You are here to learn, and part of that experience is in discovering that you are worthy and good enough. To attract love and abundance you must believe you're worthy of it and reflect it in your being. When you appreciate all of you, accepting your dark side as well as your light side, just as you are, you will feel more connected with the world and the others in it. Peace and Heaven are a state of mind. The Kingdom of Heaven is within. She may also show up as your mother or a mother figure, here or in spirit, with a message for you.

L'IMPERATORE   IV   THE EMPEROR
L'EMPEREUR   EL EMPERADOR

DER HERRSCHER   DE KEIZER

Keywords
Aries. Experience. Father figure.
Organize. Ideal Male for Female.
Discipline. Structure

The Emperor

Consciousness

Unlike The Empress Mother, The Emperor is the disciplinarian Father aspect of The Creator. He represents structure, organization and worldly experience. As opposed to the mother's nurturing energy, the archetypal father's tough love energy would be more inclined to be concerned with the education, career and financial future of his children. Was your childhood experience with your father a positive one or a negative one? How you felt about your father will effect how you feel about men and authority figures later on in life, depending on what kind of relationship you had with your father. It will also effect your ability to establish discipline, structure and organization in your life, which in turn, may effect your education, career and financial future. Unless you had a positive father experience, you will need to heal the father aspect within yourself. He can also represent a father figure or you being the father to yourself or others. For a female, the Emperor would be her ideal mate.

Counsel

The Emperor indicates a need to pay attention to your inner fathering qualities. He also reveals information about how you feel about the authority figures and governing energies you have experienced thus far in your life, which will inevitably effect your responses to others that remind you of them, positively or negatively. Ask yourself how you feel about your father and authority figures. Pay attention to what you might be attracting, based on those feelings. Are you more comfortable being a boss rather than working for one? Perhaps you need more structure, discipline and organization right now to accomplish what you desire. The Emperor might even be a father or father figure in your life, whether in spirit or here on earth, with a message he wants to give you.

IL PAPA
LE PAPE
V
THE HIEROPHANT
EL PAPA

DER HIEROPHANT
DE HIËROFANT

Keywords
Taurus. Seeking guidance. Teacher.
Counselor. Place of worship or education

The Hierophant

Consciousness

After our parents, we are exposed to the thought influences of our teachers, religious leaders and educational systems, and that is what The Hierophant represents. Has their thinking or behavior effected or changed yours? Have they used their power of influence to empower you, themselves or the organizations they represent? Have they enriched your life with their wisdom, or empowered you to think for yourself? No matter what the source, if it comes from outside yourself, take the best (what resonates with you) and leave the rest. The keys to the kingdom are within you. You are the authority and expert on yourself. Don't assume others know more than you. Always go with your intuition first.

Counsel

The Hierophant, in a reading, can come up for conventional religious systems (their belief systems, leaders and establishments), large corporations, commercial establishments (your place of employment, restaurants, bars, clubs, schools, hospitals, etc.) and anyone who is giving you professional counsel or educating you such as teachers, therapists and doctors (or lawyers and courts, when next to the Justice or Judgement cards). How has this educator, advisor or institution impacted your life positively or negatively? Have relationships in your life been effected by them? Are religious issues coming between you and another or bringing you closer together? The Hierophant will call upon you for discernment of information in many areas of your life, but in the end you must go within for what resonates with your heart and soul. Remember that the kingdom of Heaven (your peace of mind and happiness) is within. Listen to your own intuition first in all matters of life.

GLI AMANTI   VI   THE LOVERS
LES AMANTS   LOS ENAMORADOS

DIE LIEBENDEN   DE GELIEFDEN

Keywords
Gemini. Indecision. Temptation.
Relationship. Partnership. Love. Soul
Mate. Crossroad

The Lovers

Consciousness

The next evolution of influence to our thought patterns are the relationships we form - our friendships, romances and partnerships. How did you feel about your first love or relationship, or the ones after that? What impact and impressions did they form in your heart and soul? What conclusions did you form in your mind, based on your experiences with them? Were they good ones you hope to experience again or hurtful ones you've had trouble letting go of, that seem to be repeating their patterns in your life? What do you need to let go of? What do you want to find again that you might have lost? The Lovers deals with your relationships, and the choices you've made and learned from as a result of them. Did you feel true love? Were there temptations that seemed like love at the time? Are there choices you regret or corrections you need to make, to move on from them? These are the kind of issues The Lovers deals with. Ideally you must master love and forgiveness for yourself and others in order to perfect your soul and live harmoniously with others. Relationships are mirrors of the things we often don't see in ourselves or something we need to learn that our partner is bringing out in us to work on.

Counsel

Each relationship you encounter is reflecting an aspect of yourself you are learning from, or they would not be in your life. What is it in the other(s) you like or dislike? What is it you wish could change or be different? How can you work on these things within yourself to alter the vibration of your attraction and bring about a harmonious co - existence? Are you blaming or crediting another for your feelings, based on something you perceive that you or they have done? Only you can create your reality (the thoughts you allow in and give form to, which then cause the emotional feelings within you). Ideally this card represents a relationship that works well, or potentially even a soul mate. This may also represent a partnership.

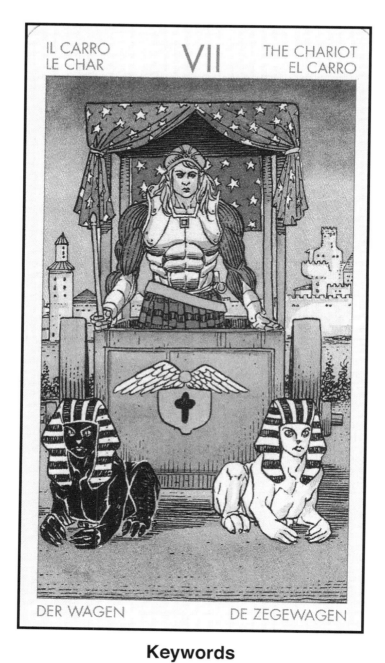

IL CARRO
LE CHAR

VII

THE CHARIOT
EL CARRO

DER WAGEN

DE ZEGEWAGEN

Keywords
Cancer. Drive. Ambition. Willfulness.
Getting spiritually centered. Car.
Travel

The Chariot

Consciousness

In our teen years, when all of life is in front of us, (and little experience has yet been gained to back it up) we tend to believe we can conquer the world in one moment and get frightened by the potential reality of it actually happening or not happening in the next. Our emotions get out of control, so we dress up and disguise our true personalities to defend ourselves and hide our vulnerabilities, so no one will see our imperfections. This consciousness is what The Chariot represents in our lives. Are you hiding who you are so no one will see your weaknesses? Do you feel the need to be perfect all the time? Do you let your emotions get out of control, letting them rule your life? Are you being pushed and pulled, back and forth by positive and negative thinking? If so, you need to get spiritually centered. An uncontrolled mind creates a life out of order. You can't control your environment but you can control your reaction based attitude to it.

Counsel

Seeing The Chariot in a reading is an indicator that you are out of control and need centering from within to bring order back into your life. Are you letting the thoughts, words and actions of others control yours? Are you trying to manipulate others with your thoughts, words and actions? Your body is the vehicle (the car) that carries and enables your soul to move about in the world of form. Your emotions are the energies (the fuel) you put in motion (e-motion) with the thoughts you let stick and allow to take form. Be mindful of the motives, intentions and planetary energies that are causing you and others you're interacting with, to react out of control. When you feel out of control yourself, remember to pause, breathe and get spiritually centered. Sometimes this card represents your car. What's happening with your car will often mirror what is going on with you as well.

Keywords

Leo. Courage. Inner strength. Seduction.
Charm. Pet. Encouragement.
Compassion. Diplomacy

Strength

Consciousness

As we grow up and gain soul maturity, we acquire the kind of compassion that comes from inner spiritual strength. The knowledge of our connection and partnership with God, as One energy ("The Father And I Are One", as Master Jesus taught), gives us the courage to tame the most Cowardly Lion (as he is symbolically represented in The Wizard of Oz). The Cowardly Lion here, is one who allows their animal ego to unleash their inner beast onto others or one's self with the intent to destroy, whether consciously or unconsciously).

Counsel

What strengths, abilities and talents do you have that will empower you to rise above your animal lower self and focus on your Divine Higher Being. Bring out the best in yourself and you will be able to do so for others as well. Your spiritual compassion and magnetism draws others to you. Be as kind to yourself as you are to others. Allow spiritual healing in, to tame where your life has gotten out of control with self sabotage, ego outbursts, or letting others affect your thoughts, actions and behaviors. Are you a healer and peacemaker or the contributer to the problem, in need of one? Healer heal thyself. Perhaps a pet to love, will comfort your soul on it's journey. Love makes the difference in the giving and receiving. Learn to co-exist with yourself and others.

L'EREMITA
L'ERMITE
IX
THE HERMIT
EL ERMITAÑO

DER EREMIT
DE KLUIZENAAR

Keywords
Virgo. Inner light. Meditation.
Spirit Guide. Therapist

The Hermit

Consciousness

At some point in life we meet someone that deeply touches our heart and soul with their compassionate wisdom. Their love and light's impact on us opens the way for us to grow as a person. They have patience for our processing of information, tolerance for our weaknesses and show genuine appreciation of who we are and the struggles that have shaped us, because they see themselves in our journey, having been there before us. With their presence in our lives we are moved to new levels of spiritual maturity. Our soul development is enriched with their ability to love. This mentor is represented by The Hermit. He also represents a point in our life when we wish to travel inward to greater heights of Self Realization ourselves, so we too, can share and lead others along the path that we have discovered.

Counsel

Your spirit guides are working with you on something they wish to bring to your attention. Important soul lessons are being presented for you to learn right now. You may be going through a period of introspection for a deeper spiritual connection to life and God. Friends, family members, and guardians, either here or on the other side may be offering their assistance to help you along your path, or on some matter of importance to you. The Hermit may also represent a therapist, teacher or good samaritan. Take time out for meditation and go within to receive the Light.

LA RUOTA   X   THE WHEEL
LA ROUE   LA RUEDA

DAS RAD   RAD VAN FORTUIN

Keywords
Jupiter. Action. Change. Luck.
What goes round comes round

The Wheel of Fortune

Consciousness

The tide comes in and the tide goes out in life. You create your own luck. Your attitude in handling each situation presented to you will be the filter that you experience the world through. Will you choose the negative path, and be reactive (the way of illusion), or the positive path of being proactive (the way of The Light)? The freewill choice you make will determine the positive or negative experiences you will learn from - suffering or joy. Life gives you the opportunities to create anew with every moment. Let go of the past and pay attention to what's directly in front of you right now. Nothing can teach you better than your own experience. All anyone else can provide for you, in their attempts to help you, is based on the filter of what they have lived and learned from. What you do with their suggestions becomes your own karma.

Counsel

You are the creator of your own reality and your own luck. The sooner you figure this out, the sooner you'll get out of the gerbil wheel of repeating the same thing over and over again. You can create anew and begin with a fresh slate, or find joy in the choices you have made that have attracted good fortune to you. Do you have the desire to learn and move forward in life now or do you need to stay back for further review? The choice is always yours. You are the only judge, jury and executioner of your life. You create it all. What you are witnessing and experiencing in the outer movie of your life right now is just a reflection of the current show in your mind's eye. Pay attention to what's playing there. What you are experiencing right now in the present is demonstrating what choices you have already made. Play, fast forward, or rewind for review. The remote control is in your hands.

Keywords
Libra. Divine Order. Fairness.
You get back what you put out.
What you sow is what you reap

Justice

Consciousness

The Karmic Law of Cause and Effect keeps Divine Order in this world. What goes 'round comes 'round. Whether your thoughts, words and actions are positive or negative determines what energy you are attracting back to yourself. You are the creator of your reality and karma. What you choose determines your fate and destiny. If you choose wrongly then you will attract what you need to correct your mistake. Choose correctly and you will attract the rewarded fruits of your efforts. Don't worry or use your vital life force focusing on who you feel has wronged you. Life is a constant balancing act of energy set in motion, so know that Divine justice will always be served.

Counsel

What is not seeming fair or just to you? Perhaps you need to view something differently, for better experiences to come your way. Are you focusing on your good to come in? What changes are you still expecting from someone else? Ask yourself as many questions as it takes to get to the root origins of your situation's solution. What beliefs did you create as a result of experiences from your past? Get it out into the open to release it. Pay close attention to what you dig up here, as it is what you've been carrying around and need to cleanse in order to move forward. If you feel you have been wronged, don't make the same mistake of choosing to be reactive. Instead, question your own point of attraction and go within for better ways for responding. What karma others attract to themselves is their responsibility. Focus on your own karma. Whatever you put out into the world will come back to you. Know in your heart that justice will prevail, for life is balanced by Divine Order.

L'APPESO
LE PENDU

XII

THE HANGED MAN
EL COLGADO

DER GEHÄNGTE   DE GEHANGENE

Keywords
Neptune. Stagnation. Illumination.
Hang ups. Sacrifice for greater cause.
Change of Perception

The Hanged Man

Consciousness

The time has arrived for you to face the life you have sacrificed, as a result of pain you weren't able to feel or deal with before. Go inward to find out what baggage you have been carrying around unconsciously, unaware of your attachments to it, and what it has been attracting into your life all this time. You must cleanse the filter of your mind from time to time, in order to gain fresh perspectives to the lessons in life, you might not have realized you were avoiding before. What are you still hanging onto? Are you blaming anyone for for your life's difficulties? Where do you need help in letting go of something or someone? A shift in perception will change your experiences as well as your level of attraction.

Counsel

The unhealed mind sets experiences into motion for you to heal yourself. Are you giving these moments your full attention? Perhaps you need to take time out to look at things differently. The benefits of letting go of old pains and letting God in, will bring you opportunities galore in help. First you must allow the Light in by turning the Light on from within. See what it is you have unconsciously held onto for so long and why. Healer heal thyself from within. Ask God to reveal whatever lesson you need to learn and for the help in learning it. You will be helped in ways you never knew were possible. You need to learn you don't have to do everything yourself and carry all your own burdens. You were never alone. You just needed to know it was safe to ask for help and the right place to request it from was God. Your spirit guides will assist you. A new way of looking at things can bring enlightenment.

LA MORTE
LA MORT

XIII

DEATH
LA MUERTE

DER TOD

DE DOOD

Keywords

Scorpio. Endings and beginnings.
Rebirth. Letting go and Letting God.
Change. Transformation. Surrender.

Death

Consciousness

With The Hanged Man, you learned to see things differently and gain a fresh new perspective on life. The Death card comes to teach us how to deal with change. We need to learn how to "Let Go and Let God". Death is not a physical death. It is a transformation from one state of being into another, preparing the way for a deep inner or outer change. When one door closes another one opens. In order for something higher and better to come into your life you must be willing to trust and surrender to a Higher Power to provide it for you. Change is eminent in life. Nothing stays the same, and the best way to handle it is to be open to the unforeseen opportunities it can offer you for personal growth.

Counsel

Be patient with the unfolding process of your journey and trust in God's timing of it. There are reasons for the changes in your experiences, even if you don't understand them. Ask for help and open your heart to let it in. Make way for your good through preparation and expectation of it, rather than keeping yourself stuck in a void of mourning what you feel you have lost. If your field of energy is filled with waves of negative thinking, there is no room to let your good in, so let go of your attachments and limitations. Believe in possibilities. Trust that there is a reason for everything.

LA TEMPERANZA XIV TEMPERANCE
LA TEMPERANCE LA TEMPLANZA

DIE MÄSSIGKEIT MATIGING

Keywords
Sagittarius. Patience. Everything in moderation, nothing in excess. One day at a time. Balancing of ingredients. Angel.

Temperance

Consciousness

At this level you are tempering the knowledge coming from the spiritual and material world to gain wisdom. We are all functioning at different levels of consciousness and understanding, as we progress up the spiritual ladder of our individual evolution. Because of this we have different points of view from one another that may or may not resonate with our own. Do your best to be patient and tolerant with others, yourself and the world. We all learn at our own speed. Try to remember this to avoid reactive, judgmental behaviors that may have consequences later on. We will all evolve at our right and perfect time. Use your intuition to know when to share with others and when to listen. Life is about learning and not about forcing your views on others. Controlling behavior comes from the ego. Learn to recognize it's presence and strive towards the awakening of your Higher Self. Balance the pros and cons of choices you are presented with to get the best outcome in all situations. Take things one day at a time to keep yourself from feeling overwhelmed and overloaded. Feel the presence of Archangel Michael's energy watching over you.

Counsel

You need to be more patient and tolerant with yourself and others. Learn what blend of ingredients will give you the desired results you are looking for, as well as when and how to apply them. Practice balancing your energy, so you won't feel overwhelmed. Your guardian angels are watching over you and guiding your efforts. Call upon them to help you. They can not intervene unless you ask for their help. Get your feet wet by stepping into the moment of the present. Sense your surroundings to gain mindful wisdom. This card could also represent opening up to your Higher Self.

IL DIAVOLO / LE DIABLE — XV — THE DEVIL / EL DIABLO

DER TEUFEL — DE DUIVEL

Keywords

Capricorn. Ego's hold on your spiritual
development. Negative emotions.
Materialism. Addictions. Perversions

The Devil

Consciousness

The Devil is not a devil "out there". The Devil card represents a consciousness of destructive, negative emotions, thoughts and behavioral patterns that cause disconnection from God and our Higher Self. It is an addictive, depressive, stuckness the Ego wants to keep you trapped in as long as it can to gain control over your energy. Allowing this in drains you of vital life force energy and causes you to feel like a powerless victim, leaving you in despair. This card indicates a need to let the Light overpower the Darkness you are holding onto. Your thoughts have gone out of control. Turn towards the Light and ask the Creator for help. Don't let destructive negative thoughts and emotions suck you in and syphon your soul.

Counsel

Block out negative thinking. Surround yourself with positive people. Energy is contagious and you don't want to be in environments or company that can suck out your positive life force with negative energy. Stay positive and see a positive opportunity in every situation, no matter how it seems at the moment. There is a gift in every adversity. Seek out the gift and allow your spirit to grow instead of being pulled down with darkness. If you are going through a tough situation call upon the Creator to send his angels to help you in overcoming it. Ask him what spiritual lesson you need to learn from the situation, and for the help and insight in learning it. Above all, stay positive and have faith that you will come through it stronger than before. The Devil also represents attachments to addictions and the illusions of materialism for happiness.

Keywords
Mars. Unexpected events. Letting go of
outworn belief systems to evolve.
Forced changes. A breaking away from
ways of before. Brainstorm

The Tower

Consciousness

The Tower is telling you to clean out the closet of your mind. Old belief systems you built on misperceptions from past memories are no longer serving you. They are now being brought up from the subconscious for cleansing. You must release the negative thought patterns that are keeping you from moving forward in life. This card is telling you to reevaluate your thinking. Get to the roots that created those faulty beliefs, or the universe will step in with further challenges to force you to dig deeper, that could be more difficult for you to deal with. This card can be an awakening of your Higher Self or a wake up call that uproots you to the core of your being. The choice is yours.

Counsel

Time to do a reality check and examine how you're thinking is effecting your life and relationships. You may need to do a Spring cleaning of the mind, as you're energy is being clouded by faulty belief systems that are no longer working for you. Sudden seemingly unexplainable changes can surface at this time or in the near future, to get you to move forward on the spiritual path. You could potentially experience an awakening or setback, depending on your readiness and willingness to evolve. Great brainstorming insights are possible this time.

LE STELLE
LES ETOILES
XVII
THE STARS
LA ESTRELLA

DER STERN
DE STER

Keywords
Aquarius. New Age. Goals. Inspiration.
Star of the show. Exposing yourself and
your talents to world.

The Star

Consciousness

Here you are tuning into your God Self and feeling more of who you truly are. You are receiving inspiration from the celestial realms. Channel Source energy down through the world of form with your particular talent. Create a rippling affect. Your vessel is being filled with the Light of The Creator, so create. Astrologically, it is a good time to reach a goal you have dreamed about achieving, and making your unique contribution to the world. Your Light has the capacity to light other Lights. Pay attention and be present to all you are sensing. It should feel like you are living in two worlds right now. A fleeting sense of heaven on earth is available to you if you go with the flow, yet stay grounded in the present.

Counsel

The time is right to let inspiration move through you, to do whatever it is you enjoy doing and you are good at. The energy is right to pursue your goals. Let your energy flow. You feel aligned with a sense of purpose. A greater force of "The Living Light" is coursing through you now. Your cup is filled, giving you energy to share and inspire others with. Others are noticing you. They sense something other worldly going on inside you, even if they don't know what it is. Use the creative force running through you to manifest your dreams.

LA LUNA
LA LUNE

XVIII

THE MOON
LA LUNA

DER MOND

DE MAAN

Keywords
Pisces. Illusion. Fear of the Unknown.
Media. Film. Computers. Internet. The
Spirit Realm. Hypnosis. Depression.
Delusional. Therapy

The Moon

Consciousness

The Moon teaches you the importance of not getting stuck in the illusions and fears that your animal nature's ego would like you to believe about yourself in the material world. Trust Spirit to help you in confronting and overcoming your fears. You have chosen to come to earth for advancing and elevating your soul. Remember your higher purpose. Your true divine nature is just borrowing and co-existing with the body you are currently dwelling in, to gain wisdom through learned experiences in the world of form. It is now time to reacquaint yourself with the Spirit World you came from, while living here on Earth. Remember where you really come from and why you are here. Learn and use the gift of your life well, while here in the physical world, as you will need to report to a counsel of elders and be graded on what you have learned and accomplished with your time here. Your report card will determine your level of soul advancement in the spirit world. Call upon your Heavenly Father. Spirit is always present to help you.

Counsel

Face your fears and don't let them run the show of your life. Both the Spirit World and Material World work together. Don't be deceived by the illusions of the Material World. Learn about the Spirit World. Get to know who you truly are and why you are here. Your life will gain greater usage and milage out of your time here by doing so. You'll feel more prepared with what to expect on the other side and be better equipped to share what you have learned and accomplished here, when going through your life review. Fear turned inward can lead to depression. Ask your fears what they have to teach you about yourself. There is nothing to fear but the fear you don't confront. It can hold you back in life, if you give your power away to it. Believe in the unseen world of spiritual guidance to help you overcome your fears and get past your comfort zone. Call upon them.

Keywords

Sun. Enthusiasm. Eternally Young Spirit.
Letting your light shine. Rewards. Bliss.
Music. Warm climate. Adventurous.
Spontaneous. Animated personality.

The Sun

Consciousness

You faced the fears of the unknown and the dark night of the soul at The Moon. Here, as a child in need, you have called upon your Heavenly Father for help, allowing the loving care of Spirit to protect and carry you through your fear. At The Sun you feel a safety, trust and bliss you didn't know before was possible, unleashing the joy and enthusiasm of your true authentic self, the divine child within you. To enter the kingdom of Heaven you must become like a child, and come to this point of trust and awareness. Like the Sun, your light is now shining brightly, with a new sense of inner power. Your energy is expanding, and the freedom to express your passion is now blossoming like the unfolding of a beautiful flower. Passion is powerful and can be directed where you would like it to go. The only limitation is the one you place on yourself. You are an heir to the Father's Throne in the Spirit World. You create with the Father's energy and give birth to your creativity in the Mother's domain, the world of form (Mother Nature). When you were born into the world you came through a physical mother. When you are born again you gain access to the Fathers' Domain, your Higher Self, to create in the Mother's World consciously.

Counsel

Listen to your inner child and give yourself the freedom to do what makes you happy. When you're happy you feel good and when you feel good you attract more to feel good about. The vibration you're transmitting will attract experiences of the same frequency back to you. To enter the kingdom of Heaven you must be like a child. Be fascinated and develop a passion for the life you were given. Ask your Creator for help when you need it. Untamed passion is like a wild horse in need of direction and training. Focus on what you want to do with it and set an intention for it with your mind. Like a child, be playful and imagine yourself enjoying the expression of your passion. Use the talents you came into this world with. Train yourself with focused concentration and practice. Let more of your true authentic self shine in the world. You will feel "light"-er.

IL GIUDIZIO
LE JUGEMENT
XX
JUDGEMENT
EL JUICIO

GERICHT
HET OORDEEL

Keywords
Pluto. Accepting consequences of your
actions. Judging or feeling judged.
Transformation. Spiritualism.
Deep spiritual inner awakening

Judgement

Consciousness

You are no longer a victim of circumstance. In actuality you never were. You just didn't know it. You allowed other people and situations to run the show of your life. You wear all the hats in the screenplay of your life and play it out on the world stage. You are the writer, director, producer, actor, audience and critic of your own movie. Excavate your history (your story) and review your life from the point of where you are today. Where do you need to forgive yourself and others for mistakes made on your journey through life? Who are you still judging or feeling judged by? Now is the time for attonement (at - one - ment). You can see the bigger picture of your life now, and resurrect yourself from any judgements you placed on yourself or others. When you heal your own life you heal the world as well.

Counsel

Where are you judging others or yourself? Where are you still feeling judged by others? Follow in the footsteps of the master teacher, Jesus. If he could say while being crucified, "Forgive them Father, they know not what they do," where can you do the same? Where in your life do you feel you have been crucified? Where in your life can you offer forgiveness for pain others caused you, knowingly or unknowingly, and where do you need to forgive yourself, for the pain you caused to others, knowingly or unknowingly? Forgive them and forgive yourself. Make the voice of your Higher Self your authority in Life. You and The Father are One. With prayer your voice is heard (communion). By meditating, you open the airwaves to listen to the Holy Spirit within you (your inner voice). Judge not and be not judged. Pray for guidance from the Father and then go inside yourself with meditation to listen for the right answers and actions.

.

IL MONDO
LE MONDE
XXI
THE WORLD
EL MUNDO

DIE WELT
DE WERELD

Keywords
Saturn. Attainment. Recognition. Travel.
Pregnancy. Childbirth. Feeling
connected and at one with the world.
Living your mission. Mediumship

The World

Consciousness

At the level of The World, you have a sense of oneness with the world. When you live consciously in the world, you see everyone and everything as a projected extension and mirror of yourself, both positively and negatively. Your life in the world can now be perceived as one huge tarot card reading. Like tarot, life in the world is symbolic, metaphoric and has patterns and cycles. At this stage you can see how everyone and everything in the world is divinely designed with absolute perfection just as it is. Spiritual messages can come to you now from anyone, anywhere and any way. You have the consciousness level to perceive life through your spiritual senses now. Having gained this wisdom, you feel connected to the life force in everyone and everything.

Counsel

You have reached a pinnacle in some lesson you needed to learn. Now is a time to be proud of yourself and your accomplishments in the world. Stay grounded in the "Now" by being aware of your surroundings. Pay attention to the hidden messages around you. Live in the world, but not of it (in consciousness). Let your mind and heart be guided by the positive, loving energy of the Higher Self and the Spirit World. Pay attention to energy. Everything and everyone is energy, including you. Learn to love and forgive everyone, including yourself. Keep an attitude of gratitude. Your life here will be so much better for it. Learn all you can and leave no lesson unturned. You don't want to go back home with baggage you will need to return with. At this level, even those who have passed on to the other side can reach you with messages, if you tune yourself into their vibration.

The Minor Arcana

The Minor Arcana

While the Major Arcana represents the spiritual lessons the soul must learn in it's travels through life, the Minor Arcana, made up of 56 cards, shows us how we will learn those spiritual lessons through our everyday experiences, trials and tribulations.

This portion of the Tarot shows us how to turn our everyday positive and negative experiences into spiritual guidance. They let us know whether we are following our best path of direction in life or not.

The minor arcana has four suits, and court cards just like a regular deck of cards. In fact it is the forerunner of our modern day playing deck. Each suit represents an aspect of our daily life: The Wands- our work, The Cups - our relationships, The Pentacles - our money and Swords - our conflicts. In a regular deck The Wands would be Clubs,The Cups would be Hearts,The Pentacles would be Diamonds and the Swords would be Spades.

The Court Cards represent both people in our lives as well as messages. The Kings represent Men, Queens represent Women, Knights represent young Men and Pages represent Babies, Children and young Women.

Wands represent: the Spring
Cups represent: the Summer
Swords represent: the Fall
Pentacles represent: the Winter

Wands represent fire signs: Sagittarius, Leo and Aries
Cups represent water signs: Pisces,Scorpio,Cancer
Swords represent air signs: Aquarius, Gemini, Libra
Pentacles represent earth signs: Taurus, Virgo, Capricorn

Wands represent: Brown/Red Hair   Cups represent: Blonde Hair
Swords represent: Gray/White Hair   Pentacles represent: Black Hair

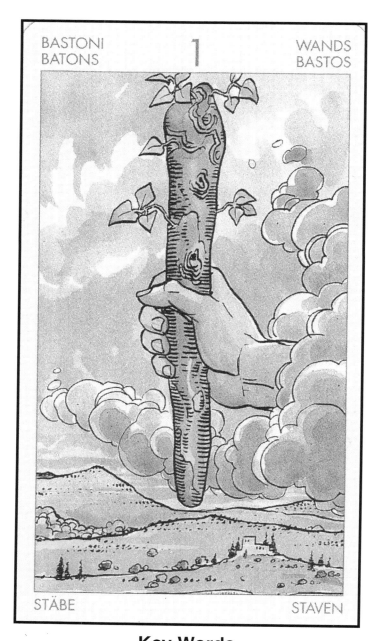

Key Words
New Ideas, jobs and projects

Springtime

Ace of Wands

Consciousness

By focusing on the positive potential in the situations and problems that are presented to you, the help and ideas needed to overcome them will appear with solutions. This could be a new job coming, the idea for an invention coming into your mind, or some other opportunity or form of assistance. "When the student is ready, the teacher appears". What this means is that when a soul is ready to learn something new, it allows the right teacher and opportunity for that education to emerge, for you to experience it.

Counsel

This card indicates a new job, invention, project or spark of enlightenment is at hand, lifting the level you have been living at. Try to keep a positive outlook in all situations presented to you, no matter what is happening, instead of letting them overcome you and keep you stuck in the negative. Life tends to test you. Be open to possibility thinking and stay in an attitude of gratitude. Remember that it's the vibration you are currently radiating that is attracting what you are experiencing and it's your thinking and feeling energy that effects your vibration, positively or negatively.

Key Words
Contemplating ideas.
Looking at options

Choices
options
- should I go this
way or that way

93

Two of Wands

Consciousness

Here you are contemplating options, opportunities and ideas going through your mind. Do you take the plunge and go after something you desire, or do you let your past and what is behind you hold you back? Decisions, decisions. This option or that one? Scarecrow, which way do I go? Will you choose to go in a new uncharted direction or a past one you're familiar with. You are comparing the pros and cons of whatever situation is in your midst- a job, relationship, location, project, etc.

Counsel

What are you feeling? What's in your gut? Fear, excitement? All the above? Can you enjoy the journey with or without your hopes and expectations being met? Change your expectations to preferences. It takes the pressure off. What are you so afraid of? If you take the plunge and just allow yourself to have the experience, can you live with it? These are the things you need to ask yourself. Are you willing to leave the safe haven of the known for the discovery of the unknown? If you look at your choices as a gamble of self discovery you can't go wrong. If your fears are getting in the way, that's the energy that will be stronger. It's all about what's in your heart and how you feel. No matter what you choose, make sure your mind is giving your heart positive messages and vice versa, because it's in your real feelings that you'll find your truest level of attraction and what's most likely to be your experience because of it.

Key Words
Planning to put ideas into action.
Daydreaming

Three of Wands

Consciousness

You're now a little closer in vibration to where you want to be. You're day dreaming about "what you can learn from your journey," more than you are about "what if something goes wrong". The "what if something goes right option" has gotten your attention and and is causing the dreaming, now going on in your head. You're beginning to get with with the program, seeing that there is nothing to lose except your own ego's desire to hold you back from life's experiences. Now you're in the creating state of consciousness, at least in terms of planning a course of action and seeing positive possibilities.

Counsel

Create the reality you wish to see by training your mind to create it. What your mind can believe, it can conceive. What is around you has already manifested into being. When you believe something is possible, the opportunities to see it will manifest in your experiences. Close your eyes and fantasize. Get your mind to work for you. Then when you can see it in your mind, make plans on how you are going to achieve it. Make a blueprint for action now, to turn your desire into reality. Decide the "whats" and the "whens", and the universe will help you orchestrate the "hows".

Key Words
Secure foundation.
Ideas firmly established.
Home. Business. Wedding

Four of Wands

Consciousness

At this junction you've either established the foundation of a dream you wanted to manifest or you're focusing on the life you have created up until now. It's time to examine your creation and do a reality check. Is this what you want? Are you happy, comfortable and secure with the life experience you've created? If you want your creation to continue as is, your focus is now on maintaining and nurturing what you have established, in the hope of keeping it going as is. If it isn't what you want, you will need to reevaluate your choices and point of focus.

Counsel

Where are you now on the "feeling" scale? Are you comfortable and enjoying the life or situation you have created? How much do you really want it, and is it enough for you to want to nurture and maintain it? What do you need to bring to the table to keep things enjoyable, harmonious and secure? What will you do to secure this thing you wanted enough to create it? Are you content with things as they are, or are there things in need of change or expansion?

| BASTONI BATONS | 5 | WANDS BASTOS |
| STÄBE | | STAVEN |

Key Words
Inner conflict. Competition. Arguments.
Conflicting ideas. Get focused

Chang
— Inner conflict
person needs to focus
the energy.

99

Change

Five of Wands

Consciousness

Conflicting ideas and desires are emerging at this stage. Do you want this or do you want that? You are sending out mixed messages to the universe, which is going to get you mixed results. Get focused. Which thoughts and actions will bring you happiness? Sometimes it takes conflicting thoughts and ideas to create greater successes and bigger ideas. Sometimes it takes hearing out these competing thoughts, to know the current wants that your soul is seeking to feel good. At this stage you have to work out the kinks in your mind and get clear on what you truly want in order to create a smooth seam of messages going out into the universe.

Counsel

Get focused. What conflicting thoughts are getting in the way of your happiness? What do you need to clear up in your mind that's disturbing your stream of consciousness and flow of manifesting? What change in communication within yourself must you work on, to establish harmony in the outer experiences you're attracting? Don't look to change others you feel are not meeting what you're wanting. They are perfectly placed in front of you, doing their job of mirroring the level you need to learn from, that you would otherwise miss out on seeing. You may want to be at another level of attraction, but this is where you are, till you change your current level of consciousness. Those conflicts you are facing right now may be gifts in disguise, revealing hidden subconscious areas you are still focusing on. Use what you don't want in your experiences, to discover what you do want, and then focus on what you want. This method allows contrast to serve your Higher Self.

Key Words
Victory. Job well done

Six of Wands

Consciousness

With the Five of Wands, you let yourself get discouraged when things didn't seem to go your way. At The Six of Wands you've taken the higher road, and chosen to clear the adversity from your mind. Now is the time to get into the vibration of accomplishments you can feel proud of. Compete with your own self and your own fears. Here you have succeeded in changing conflicting thoughts and experiences that existed in your mind and actions before and have reaped the rewards in your outer experiences as a result. Continue this positive stream of consciousness you are currently creating from. You are on track with what's working and "feeling good". Others are noticing your success as well.

Counsel

You have made the right choice of getting positively focused on possibilities, not letting the competition of your own inner conflicts stand in your way. It's time to pat yourself on the back for taking the higher road less traveled - a victory for your Higher Self. It's time to reap the benefits and rewards. Be an example for others to follow.

BASTONI BATONS — 7 — WANDS BASTOS

STÄBE — STAVEN

Key Words
Self doubt. Trust yourself

Not trusting your
intutation
— your Doubting
yourself

—You can handle
what is coming
your way

103

Seven of Wands

Consciousness

Uh oh! You are letting self doubt get in your way again. The old fears and negative thought patterns from your subconscious are coming back to haunt you and are causing you to feel that you can't handle the task in front of you. Trust your instincts and know that you can handle whatever is coming at you. You're getting closer to your passions being realized and perhaps it's scary to be Big, but be the hero to yourself and show what you've got.

Counsel

Believe in yourself, your ideas, and your skills and get get rid of that old pattern of self doubt. You have everything you need to do whatever you want. Your instincts are very good, yet you are still showing inner uncertainty. Work on trusting your instincts and keep on going after what you want, by staying on top of things.

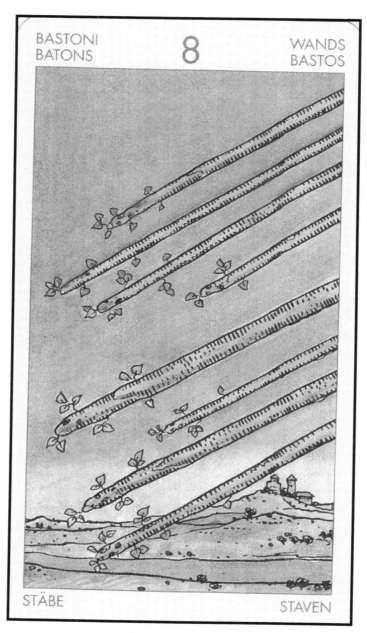

BASTONI
BATONS
8
WANDS
BASTOS

STÄBE
STAVEN

Key Words
ESP. Ideas soon to manifest.
Communication coming or going out.
Travel by airplane

Intuation
right on

Travel over a Body
of water

105

Eight of Wands

Consciousness

The energy of your current thoughts and emotions have gone out into the ethers already, soon to meet their vibrational match in manifestation. Pay attention and look inward for the hows and whys things are showing up on your radar. Learn from what you've created in your reality. See where you can make improvements. Use your intuition to figure out what you've set in motion, consciously or unconsciously, and why. The reason is not in others or outside events. You are the cause of your attraction, making you a powerful creator.

Counsel

News is going out or coming in that you have set into motion. Something you want could be on it's way to you, so be patient with the process. Any spiritual work you've been doing on yourself has opened you up psychically. Be open to intuitive messages coming in from the universe and trust your instincts in receiving them. Pay attention to your surroundings as this is the barometer of where you are on the attraction scale of creating, whether positively or negatively. Remember, it's all good / all God. Learn what you do want from what you don't want. The universe is impersonal and gives you what you cause into being by the thoughts, words and actions you are vibrating at.

Key Words
Defending ideas. Stand up for yourself

Speak up for yourself.

Nine of Wands

Consciousness

You may feel you have been taken advantage of or feel you need to defend yourself in a situation. Ask yourself what you need to learn about yourself via what thoughts, words and actions you've set in motion (consciously or unconsciously) that have caused this current reality your in. You've been through the mill. You must ask yourself, are you going to allow yourself to feel defeated by the circumstances facing you? Stand up for yourself or chalk it up to one of life's learning experiences and let it go. Only you really know what's the best choice for your soul's development.

Counsel

You may need to take a stand, speak up and defend yourself. Don't allow others to bully, brow beat or intimidate you with their energy, words or actions. Look inward as to why you're attracting this into your reality. Where do you need to get stronger? No one is any more secure or superior than you are. They have either had more experience in the area of life where you find yourself now, or they are mighty fine actors who want to make you believe they've got their act together. Don't buy into the hype. Everyone is selling what they want others to see about themselves, in order to get their own needs met. If you don't feel so strong, fake it till you make it. Face your fear or guilt and let it teach you to love yourself more. Remember, you're the creator of your reality. When you love and understand yourself more, you'll have more love and understanding to give others.

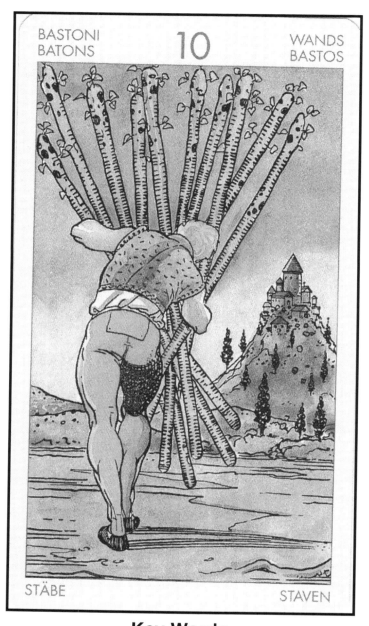

Key Words
Burdens. Too many thoughts on
mind or things to do. Pressure.
Feeling overwhelmed

Ten of Wands

Consciousness

At the present time you're overwhelmed by too much on your mind or too much work ahead of you to meet your expectations of yourself, or the ones you feel others may have of you. You need to lighten up and find what it is that will make you feel good and happy right now, otherwise you're going to attract more of what you're currently vibrating at. Tell yourself "I want to feel good". Sing, listen to music or something that will allow your mind some relaxation. Say some positive affirmations. Look inward. Where in your history have you carried more than your share of burdens? What beliefs are you still hanging onto that are still attracting the experience of feeling burdened?

Counsel

You need to lighten your load, take a break and find a way to do things smarter instead of harder. You're mind or schedule is way too overloaded. Pray for help. Ask and you will receive. Spirit can't intervene unless you ask. Don't worry. Worry only attracts more to worry about, because that's the energy frequency you are broadcasting at. Go out and get some fresh air. Take a breather away from what you're doing. Turn on the TV, pick up a book, spend a few moments with friends on the phone or grab a snack. Then come back to what you're doing with a mind that is more refreshed. Your sense of commitment to getting your work done will eventually pay off, but right now you need some time out, so you won't burn yourself out.

FANTE DI BASTONI   KNAVE OF WANDS
VALET DE BATONS   SOTA DE BASTOS

BUBE DER STÄBE   STAVEN SCHILDKNAAP

Key Words
Contemplation of some
kind of message, news or contract.
Baby, Young Child , Girl.

Beginnings

message by
paper

– contract,
– resume,
– application

111

Page of Wands

Consciousness

This card has you contemplating some new idea or one that's already in motion, but with a fresh new outlook. A stream of consciousness could be entering your mind for observation. If you're waiting for results in the mail of something you have put into motion, it could very well be showing up soon. Think positively to attract positively. It could even be a contract you're contemplating getting for business, or a partnership you want to make or break apart from.

Counsel

Put your ideas to paper, write that book or resume, and see the outcome of your desire or situation realized and manifested in your mind, to speed up the process. Focus your thoughts on paper or on your computer, and send that email, invitation or resume out to whomever it is you want to say something to. This could also be your contemplation of what someone else has written to you before you send back a reply. Think positive. Your energy can be felt by others whether in form, word or thought. Energy knows no distance. You may be receiving some message, invitation or important news soon. A contract of some kind may be in the midst of coming, or waiting to be considered and signed.

CAVALLO DI BASTONI   KNIGHT OF WANDS
CHEVALIER DE BATONS   CABALLO DE BASTOS

RITTER DER STÄBE   STAVEN RIDDER

Key Words
Putting ideas into action.
Job changes. Young man

getting jobs

– Get up and do
something

113

Knight of Wands

Consciousness

You've got an idea and you're running with it. You can't wait to share it with someone else to get the feedback or results you are hoping for. You're mind is constantly changing with exciting ideas. Nothing is going to keep you down. Passion is fueling you're thoughts into action. You're enjoying what you are learning from all of your adventures, and sharing them with others. Your mind is alive and alert with a constant flow of ideas running through your head. Be open to it all. A stream of consciousness is coming on strong. You might want to write it down while the flow is there.

Counsel

Action and adventure are on the horizon for you. New and exciting changes are in your midst to learn from.... your job, where you are living, etc. You are going after your dreams and making yourself available to all kinds of opportunities as a result. The universe is talking to you and you are going with the flow. Nothing can hold you down. You're putting your ideas into action.

REGINA DI BASTONI   QUEEN OF WANDS
REINE DE BATONS   REINA DE BASTOS

KÖNIGIN DER STÄBE   STAVEN KONINGIN

Key Words
Sidetracked by emotions or
subconscious. Woman

20-up
30-up

— Don't let your
emotions side track
you what you are going to do

115

Queen of Wands

Consciousness

It's tempting right now to get sidetracked by all the old familiar tapes and emotions that want to distract you from your higher purpose. Going in the direction of your Higher Self can mean a lot of commitment. Are you ready for all that comes with this path? You've been growing at a pretty fast pace and now taking time out to digest it all. Don't fall prey to the emotions your ego would like to trip you up with, making you believe you can't handle what you've set out to do. You've come so far in your journey. Others can see your inner strengths and beauty. You must learn to see them as well.

Counsel

People look up to you and respect your passion, acquired spiritual wisdom and good naturedness. You tend to have a positive effect on all those who come into contact with you. Don't let the constant inner chatter of your own subconscious emotions distract you from who you are and what you want to do. Keep pushing yourself forward, inspire others with your inner beauty and reach for your full potential. Focus on your growth and the opportunities that lie ahead of you. Maximize the positives and minimize the negatives that want to get in your way. Use your talents to create.

Key Words
Projecting ideas to others
and future. Man

— what it's
gonna feel like
— where this idea
can go

117

King of Wands

Consciousness

You're able to project your ideas into the future. From observation, you've learned which ideas work and which ones don't. You're a powerful and persuasive leader with magnetic appeal. Others are drawn to you. Ideas flow endlessly through your head, due to a deep connection with Spirit. You can be very persuasive with that creative mind and passionate attitude of yours. You are deeply entrenched in your concept, with the finished product of your idea executed to creation, already digesting in your head.

Counsel

There is a magnetic, seductive charm to your nature that makes people listen when you speak. You have no problem getting others to see your point of view. You have proactively taken your mind into the past and future to know how to project your ideas into the present. You're earned wisdom makes you a good observer of what will work in your favor and get the results you desire.

COPPE
COUPES
1
CHALICES
COPAS

KELCHE
BEKERS

Key words
New attitudes, values, feelings and
relationships. Summer.

Ace of Cups

Consciousness

You are the Holy Grail receiving the Light, Love and Living Waters of the Holy Spirit into your vessel. Source energy is filling your Sacred Heart with a blissful experience of unconditional love. You are a source of light to all those you are coming into contact with and deeply effecting many lives. People feel your energy and want to be around the glow they feel radiating from you. You are attracting new relationships into your life now, and elevating existing ones to new levels of intimacy or commitment.

Counsel

The Holy Spirit has touched your heart and soul deeply from within. A state of blissful joy is accompanying the higher consciousness you are currently experiencing. The unconditional love energy you are generating is drawing windows of opportunity for new love relationships, friendships and partnerships to be attracted to you, and existing ones to strengthen now. People feel your light and want to be around you. You are glowing from within and touching the lives of others with your light.

COPPE
COUPES

2

CHALICES
COPAS

KELCHE

BEKERS

Key Words
Communication. Creating
harmonious relationships.

Two of Cups

Consciousness

See the eyes of God in all you come into contact with. Learn from your interactions with others and look for what you can appreciate in them, as well as in yourself. Be a conscious observer of what each relationship experience you come into contact with has to offer you for your growth. You are drawn together to learn something about yourselves you might otherwise not be aware of. Accept the fact that each person, including yourself, is exactly where they need to be for what they need to learn. Be patient with the process and you will go a long way in making friends and creating bonds that will enrich your life.

Counsel

Make the most out of your relationships now. See what the person you're interacting with has to teach you about being a better you, be it romantic, friendship or partnership. Every relationship we have is a mirror of something we generally don't recognize in ourselves. They reflect back to us the areas we need to work on. Everyone you come into contact with is projecting something you need to learn about your inner world. Look for the good and you will find more of it. Find fault and you will find more of that. You choose.

COPPE
COUPES
3
CHALICES
COPAS

KELCHE
BEKERS

Key Words
Happiness. Socializing. Groups.
Parties. Gatherings
gossip

Three of Cups

- creation *- emotions*

Consciousness

People enjoy your light filled, joyous presence and you enjoy theirs. It's a time to be social and share the light with others. The positive energy you're creating is contagious and beneficial to all. The happiness you have benefited from in your relationships has spread further, to create harmonious group involvements. Be fruitful in your joy and multiply the energies wherever you go and meet with others. Go out and enjoy yourself.

Counsel

Create happiness for yourself and others wherever you are, and there you will always find it. Build a momentum of joy and share your love and light. Be the energy you wish to attract and the Law of Attraction will magnetize it to you with like minded souls. Be out in the presence of others who have the kind of energy you wish to enjoy, especially those that have interests in common with you. You blend your energy with others, just as they do with you. Keep your energy positive to strengthen your vibrational field. Don't let other's energy influence you, if it doesn't mesh with who you are, and the person you wish to be. If something or someone feels "off", trust your instinct and stay true to yourself.

Key Words
Be more conscious of what's around you

Someone hard to talk too.
In their own little world

125

Four of Cups

Consciousness

In the joy and momentum of the three of cups party mode, you may have missed or overlooked some important things you needed to pay attention to, that you now need to learn from in retrospect. Maybe something was said or done that hurt your feelings before, that you weren't expecting to deal with. "Those big bad mean people did stuff to me - victim thinking" could be moving through your mind here. Maybe you hurt someone else's feelings and don't understand why. You now need to get yourself together in self reflection, before mingling with others again, to regain your happiness or peace of mind. In any case, it's a time for retreat and introspection.

Counsel

Take some time out to go within. Don't judge, just observe. What is going on inside? Ask yourself questions. Do a reality check on what's happening in your current situation or environment. What opportunities are there that you might be missing out on, or need to learn from? In order to build your energy field back up again you need to go inward with self reflection now for insight.

Hiding your light under your Dark Shadow.

—Anything you are focusing on your recycling more 6 that energy.

Key Words
Regrets over past.
Be grateful for the life you do have

— Don't hold on to regrets

try to learn something positive over something negative

Five of Cups

Consciousness

Perhaps you've gone overboard in the time you've spent in the introspection mode of consciousness. Here you've entered "pity party" thinking and gone into worry wart mode. "Woe is me, they've done me wrong, poor me, nobody loves me, no sense trying again, cause I'll just get hurt all over again" type of thinking is causing much emoting. You're in the "I coulda, shoulda, woulda, but it's too late now" zone. Can't put spilled milk back into the bottle. You need to let go of past regrets and focus on the things you have to feel grateful for. Remember whatever you're thinking about is vibrating it's energy frequencies out there. The Law of Attraction is impersonal and will magnetize back to you more of whatever you are thinking about. It is Law. You want to focus on whatever you can to feel good right now, even if it's to love yourself no matter how you feel. Even that is a step in the right direction.

Counsel

Earth is a schoolhouse for learning. It's time to change your focus and redirect your precious, God given, life energy in a better way. Don't stay negatively focused on the "coulda, shoulda, woulda", "he/she has done me wrong" mindset. Turn things around for yourself energetically, by redirecting your attention to what is going right, instead of what is or has gone wrong. Focus your mind on things that you can be grateful for, to elevate your vibration. This will improve your level of attraction. Things could have been worse and it wasn't as bad as it could have been, because you're still alive and things can still change. With God anything is possible, so get into an attitude of gratitude. Tell yourself you want to " feel good".

COPPE
COUPES
6
CHALICES
COPAS

KELCHE
BEKERS

Key Words
Pleasant memories of the past.
Deja Vue. Past Life

Soul mate

Six of Cups

Consciousness

Memories of happier times you had, or wanted to have, from your past are surfacing. Use these memories to propel yourself forward and gain from it what you can in the present. It's very possible, with this card to have a past life recall or a sense of deja vue with someone, or something showing up in your present life or present moment. Listen to the voice of your inner child, with the six of cups. She or he may be trying to get your attention, to be heard. It's very important to listen.

Counsel

Don't let thinking about how things were in the past, ruin your precious moments in the present. Create a fresh slate to start where you are planted right now in the present. Relish the happy moments you had in the past, or forgive and let go of the fantasy of thinking how things could have been any different then they were. Ask Spirit to help you overcome what is keeping you stuck in the past, that is now interfering with your ability to move forward. Ask for the help you need to release and let go of your attachments to any memories still causing you pain. Focus on the positive things you have overcome, things that have strengthened the person you have become, and let go of anything negative thinking still lingering. Champion yourself now by giving yourself anything you feel you have missed out on. Another thing that could be happening at this time is that you might be reuniting with someone from your past. A reunion could be coming up soon. You might also sense a strong sense of deja vue with someone in your present midst. This person may be a reacquaintance you knew from a previous life. This card also indicates you may have a need to work with your inner child.

COPPE
COUPES
7
CHALICES
COPAS

KELCHE
BEKERS

positive

Key Words
— Imagination. Confusion

∪negative

possibilites

Any # of possibilit,
— so many choices
— worry - Department too

131

Seven of Cups

Consciousness

Here you are becoming aware of how the thoughts impressed on your subconscious mind are creating together with your conscious mind, both positively and negatively. You must tend the garden of your mind. Weed out the negative thoughts you don't want to take root and spread. Plant the seeds of positive thoughts you wish to grow. How are you using your imagination? Are you creating consciously or unconsciously? This is the time to pay attention to what's going on in your imagination. Your thoughts are creating your reality all the time. Even when you think you are not choosing, you are still choosing, unconsciously. Rather than using your imagination to worry about the "what ifs", use your imagination to visualize the reality you want to create in your life.

Counsel

Use the power of your imagination to visualize and direct your energy consciously. What would you like to create in your life experiences? Train your subconscious to go in the direction you would like it to manifest. Close your eyes and fantasize. Make a vision board - a treasure map of your wishes, to help you visualize. Use positive affirmations. Get your mind out of the worry zone. Worry is a negative way of using your power to create and so, in essence, it is a negative prayer. Be the powerful, positive creator you were born to be. You were born in the Image of the Creator to Co-Create.

COPPE
COUPES

8

CHALICES
COPAS

KELCHE

BEKERS

Key Words
Going into the unknown. Soul searching

time to yourself
connect w/spirit

Eight of Cups

Consciousness

At the 7 of cups you were made aware of the power of your imagination, and it's effects on the reality you are creating, both consciously and subconsciously. You're now ready to go to the next stage of your journey, to the inner worlds of your being, and do some serious soul searching. It's time to go inward and see how you got to where you are in the present. Learn about who you are, what life has taught you about yourself and why you have created your past and current experiences. There was a reason you drew those experiences to yourself. They have provided you with the unique, valuable wisdom that only you, yourself, have experienced. Use this wisdom to help yourself create what you want in your reality, moving forward into the present and future.

Counsel

Take time alone right now to go inward and do some serious soul searching. Listen to the wisdom of your Higher Self. Find out what it is about your energy and life experiences that makes you who you are and makes your experience in the world uniquely yours. Become the authority of your own observations. Only you can really know what it's like to live life in your shoes. Don't let what others think and feel get in the way of your own experienced wisdom. Use your past and present experiences to know more about what you need and want to fulfill your dreams.

COPPE
COUPES

9

CHALICES
COPAS

KELCHE

BEKERS

Key Words
Wishes coming true.
Be careful what you wish for.

Wish
Card

135

Nine of Cups

Consciousness

You've gone through the soul searching stage at the eight of cups, to know what you wish for, and now with the nine of cups, you have gained the wisdom from within yourself, to create it into being. By setting forth conscious intentions of your desired wishes to the Source of Creation, the Universe can now respond and bring it to you. Your emotions are the equivalent of commands. The stronger the intensity of your emotions, (caused by your thoughts) the stronger the forcefield of energy frequencies there are to bring forth your desires. Doubt weakens the energy field of your intensions, so train your mind, and strengthen your thoughts with practice over and over. Start with small believable intentions and then build to greater ones. You must train your mind to work for you, with concentrated practice, over and over, till it becomes a part of you. This card is known as the wish card. Wish big. Nothing is impossible if you believe it can happen.

Counsel

Focus on what you want. Set intentions. The more you believe you will receive what you ask the universe for, the more likely you are to attract it to yourself, in just about any way. Spirit will orchestrate the ways to get it to you. Use positive affirmations, self hypnosis tapes, vision boards, visualization....basically anything it takes to convince yourself that you can have what you want and get your mind working for you. Know you are worthy and deserving of your desires, and get rid of doubt. Believe in yourself and your dreams. Practice setting and saying your intentions over and over again, till you achieve the results you are seeking. Expand your vision of who you are. You are energy in motion and made in the image of your Creator. God said (with intention), "Let there be light" and there was light.

COPPE
COUPES
10
CHALICES
COPAS

KELCHE
BEKERS

Key Words
Happiness and contentment for all

= people pleaser
wants to be
loved by
everybody

- peacemaker

Happy ever after
ending

Ten of Cups

Consciousness

Somewhere over the rainbow dreams really do come true. The Light of God is shining down upon you for a job well done in manifesting your dreams, and for creating your happiness. You have managed to hold the thoughts of your desires long enough to see them realized before you. The signs of your success are everywhere. You are now consciously Co- Creating with your Creator, and have much to feel grateful for. You are a magnet for the things that make your heart sing, because happiness breeds more happiness and gratitude brings more things to be grateful for. Continue to live from your heart and be a model for others to do the same.

Counsel

Happiness is what you make it to be. It's a place in your heart and a positive mental outlook that makes your spirit feel more alive. Enjoy the life you've created. Be grateful for what you have and you will have more to be grateful for. Focus on what's good in everything and everyone, including yourself and you will find more good to experience life with. Live from your heart and trust your emotions to guide you now. Life is good. Life is God. When you feel good you feel God.

FANTE DI COPPE   KNAVE OF CHALICES
VALET DE COUPES   SOTA DE COPAS

BUBE DER KELCHE   BEKERS SCHILDKNAAP

Key Words
Surprise messages. Phone calls.
Pay attention to feelings.
Baby, Young Child, Girl.

Beginning)

139

Page of Cups

Consciousness

Be open to receiving messages from the universe, from just about any person, place, or thing, by staying present in the moment. It could be a phone call from someone you were just thinking of, a song playing in the store you just happened to be in, or something over the radio while you're driving in the car. Make yourself an open vessel to receive from spirit, by getting rid of any unnecessary stuff clogging your mind. Allow answers and solutions to what you have been asking for to come in, and they will, sometimes very unexpectedly and by surprise.

Counsel

Practice being in the moment, and making yourself available to spiritual messages, that are ever present when you're tuned in. Your spirit guides may be trying to make you aware of something in these messages. A phone call or offer could be coming from someone you need to or wish to hear from. Pay attention to opportunities coming in, including new feelings that need your attention. Expect the unexpected.

CAVALLO DI COPPE   KNIGHT OF CHALICES
CHEVALIER DE COUPES   CABALLO DE COPAS

RITTER DER KELCHE   BEKERS RIDDER

Key Words
Proceeding slowly but surely. Offers.
Change in feelings, young man

no rush to getting anywhere

141

Knight of Cups

changes (handwritten)

- water sign (handwritten)
- hair color Blonde (handwritten)

Consciousness

Proceed with conscious awareness and caution. Pay attention to your feelings and emotions, as a barometer of what you want and don't want to experience, before moving forward on offers coming in at this time. If something feels good, go with it, but if it doesn't, hold back and wait, or make changes. There is some uncertainty in your feelings, as to whether you are treading on the right or wrong path at this time. Listen to your gut instinct and trust the inner guidance of your soul.

Counsel

Go at a slow pace that allows you to observe what you are feeling, before making assessments and moving forward on opportunities coming your way right now. Trust your intuition on how to proceed in all choices you are making, personally and professionally, at this time. You could be feeling a change of heart about something, someone or some location. Ask your spirit guides for help in knowing how to proceed.

REGINA DI COPPE   QUEEN OF CHALICES
REINE DE COUPES   REINA DE COPAS

KÖNIGIN DER KELCHE   BEKERS KONINGIN

Key Words
Visualizing. Intuition. Over imagining.
Mother figure, woman

—Visualize

—Someone who
   worries

— highly
  intuitive

Mother Card

143

Inner word

Queen of Cups

Consciousness

Your power of imagination, visualization and intuition will in many cases give you psychic abilities and artistic talents. You have a motherly quality about you that makes you want to nurture others, however you can also be overly sensitive and moody or reactive at times. You have a giving heart but your heart can easily get hurt as well, since you risk being open, to live life more fully. You tend to be deeper than most, however your innocent desire to love and be loved can cause you to be somewhat unbalanced in the area of trust at times. Negative use of your imagination can cause you to worry too much at times. Your compassionate nature has you endeared by the hearts of many.

Counsel

Your sensitivity gives you a loving nature and inner beauty, but when you let your emotional nature get affected by ego (others, as well as your own) you can easily become reactive and become the cause of emotional pain (to yourself, as well as others). Learn to become proactive and detached from the ego. This can be done by observing life as a schoolhouse of spiritual lessons. With this perception in mind, your Divine Nature can see it's all good and all God, no matter what you're feeling, allowing you to be more peaceful in your experiences. You are often quite gifted with psychic abilities and artistic talents.

RE DI COPPE   KING OF CHALICES
ROI DE COUPES   REY DE COPAS

KÖNIG DER KELCHE   BEKERS KONING

Key Words
Projecting into life what may
or may not come to pass, man

— projecting their
feelings

—

water sign man
— guy w/ Blonde hair
— water sign

145

King of Cups

Consciousness

You're quite sensitive and intuitive. Although you are a kind soul by nature, your emotional sensitivity makes it uncomfortable for you to feel so openly vulnerable with others. When you act out unconsciously, you tend to project your feelings and insights, good or bad, onto others, unaware of the energies you are reverberating back to yourself. You can be rather moody at times. You must learn not to let ego cause your idealistic, spiritual nature to become imbalanced by your sensitive nature, if you want others to appreciate your insights. You are a deep and gentle soul who is generally quite spiritual and liked by others.

Counsel

You are generally a kind, gentle and spiritual soul that most people feel comfortable being around. You can show a very warm heart or be rather emotionally reactive to others, when influenced by ego (yours or others) due to your sensitivity. There are many levels to your soul that others don't always see. You can be a very moody and somewhat complicated being, causing you to be misunderstood by others. You are often quite gifted with psychic abilities and artistic talents.

SPADE
EPEES

1

SWORDS
ESPADAS

SCHWERTER

ZWAARDEN

Key Words
Taking new action
to overcome problems

147

Ace of Swords

Consciousness

There is nothing you can't conquer right now. The force is with you! The strength of your conviction and energy make this an ideal time to go after a problem that is in your midst. You have the right mental attitude and have the inner strength to go after it. Cut through that wheat and get rid of that chaff. By now you've gained enough power and might to overcome whatever hurdles you might have had standing in your way before. Be proactive. Now is not the time to put things off.

Counsel

Take care of whatever problems you are facing right now. Don't procrastinate and wait till things grows and get out of hand. Don't slack off and hope that someone else will do the job for you. Take charge of your destiny and fight your own battles. Don't let others pull a fast one over you and get away with things that have hurt you, leaving you drained of energy. Be a spiritual warrior and go after the unjust! Take the initiative to solving whatever is troubling you. The force of your energy and the strength of your conviction right now make this a great time to take charge of things in need of your attention.

SPADE EPEES 2 SWORDS ESPADAS

SCHWERTER ZWAARDEN

Key Words
Unable to accept reality
or something going on

Two of Swords

Consciousness

Something you are going through right now is just too difficult for you to accept and handle, but keep the faith. Eventually you will have grown stronger from having endured and gone through the experience. It's OK for it to not be OK right now. Whatever you are experiencing feels just too unbearable to come to terms with at the moment. You may not always like what you're getting and experiencing here in Earth School, but you'll always get what you need to move forward spiritually. Perhaps someday, when you have overcome this time in your life, you will be able to help someone else going through a similar situation, by telling your story.

Counsel

Take some time out to let your heart heal from whatever is causing you pain. Hang in there. This too shall pass away. When the time is right and your emotions have had the time to acclimate to your situation, you can be strong again and rise up again, like the phoenix out of the fire, being stronger than you ever imagined yourself capable of before. Only you know when that time is. Don't let other's opinions rule and effect your thoughts, unless it feels helpful. They haven't lived your experiences and don't have all the answers they may think they do. They may be more hurtful then helpful, regardless of their intentions. They too are human and their motives aren't always as good or as bad as you think.

SPADE EPEES · 3 · SWORDS ESPADAS

SCHWERTER ZWAARDEN

Key Words
Disappointment or heartbreak.

Three of Swords

Consciousness

Your heart is hurting from pain that seems unbearable. Maybe it's a breakup of a romance or partnership. Perhaps you are going through a separation or divorce. Maybe you have lost someone or something dear to your heart. It could even be a betrayal of trust by someone you thought was there for you. It's important now to walk through the feelings and deal with the situation at hand. Know that God, The Creator loves you and will help you in your time of need. You can turn this around and make it work for you, with faith and the right mental attitude. Focusing on the pain with blame will just bring more of the same and keep you stuck longer. Hang in there. Better times will come.

Counsel

Call upon God, your spirit guides, and the angels to assist you. They can not intervene unless you ask for help first. It's important now more than ever to believe that help from Spirit is always there for you. Call upon help from others around you if you can. Trust that life is a process. All of your experiences, no matter how hard they may seem at the time, are in your life for a reason. There is a gift in every adversity. When you are ready, you will find it.

Key Words
Rest, meditation and prayer

Four of Swords

Consciousness

Here you need to rest, regroup and gain inner security, away from stress. Your mind and body are in need of refreshment and revitalization. Meditation is an especially important tool for tuning into spirit guides who can help you. It also strengthens the current of your energy field and light body. Pay attention to your dreams. Important messages could be coming in. This card is a reminder to pray, meditate and get some rest and relaxation.

Counsel

The wisest thing to do right now is to get some rest and relaxation. Then go inward. Meditation, prayer, positive reframing of your mind, and affirmations are the way to go here. You need some time out from the stress of daily life. Take a nap or go to sleep. Jot down your dreams. Friends and family on the Other Side might have something they want you to tell you. Take some time out for yourself to heal or regroup from within, and charge up your battery.

Key Words
Conflict. Communication problems

Five of Swords

Consciousness

Taking your anger and frustration out on others is attracting the same energy right back to you like a boomerang. The problem is in your attitude or you wouldn't be attracting what you are here. Blaming and accusing others for your problems will make enemies and cause you to lose friends, if you stay on this road of reacting badly to others. No one likes to be accused, bullied or intimidated. Maybe someone in your life has done this to you somewhere in your past, but it's not the answer to handling your problems now. The only way to win in communication is when the others you are interacting with come away feeling they're point of view has been heard as well. If someone has been treating you badly in some way, know it will come back to them. Being proactive rather than reactive will get you better results in handling conflicts with others. Try to find the middle ground.

Counsel

Don't burn bridges behind you. Build new ones that allow everyone to grow. Hurting others because you have been hurt before is no excuse for bad behavior. It will come back to haunt you later by boomeranging right back to you, with negative karma. It serves no one to dump negative energy onto others by venting out. Don't let others get your goat and cause you to react. Pause, breathe deeply and respond from a higher energy of spiritual maturity. Love yourself for where you're at, with all your flaws and defects, instead of projecting your problems and negativity onto others. Don't allow others to dump their problems on you either. This card usually indicates communication problems that need to be resolved.

SPADE
EPEES
6
SWORDS
ESPADAS

SCHWERTER
ZWAARDEN

Key Words
Difficulties leaving. Travel.
Changing location

Six of Swords

Consciousness

Difficulties are leaving you. Perhaps you are moving away from a difficult situation that could not be peacefully resolved after doing your best to work things out. Either way, you've made progress and gone with choices in thought and action that will better serve you. You're experiencing more harmonious energy from moving in the right direction. Sometimes you just have to cut your losses, see them as life's lessons, or paying off a karmic debt, and move forward. This could be one of those times. It's time to turn life's lemons into cosmic lemonade, so to speak. Take what you have learned from overcoming life's difficulties and turn them into something good.

Counsel

It's time to move forward, and away from a negative mindset. Some difficult situations you have come across recently or in the past are being processed now with right thinking. Smoother times lie ahead of you because of this. If you can allow your mind to see what you've gone through as moving through life's lessons, or paying off a karmic debt, you will be in the flow of right energy and see relief in your experiences. Might be a good time to take a trip (or just get away from your current environment for awhile) and refresh your mind, from the energies of a different location.

SPADE / EPEES / 7 / SWORDS / ESPADAS

SCHWERTER / ZWAARDEN

Key Words
Creating problems for yourself.
Get out of your own way. Dishonesty
Self sabotage. Sneak thief. Cheater

Seven of Swords

Consciousness

You feel cheated by someone or something that has happened to you and you can't get it off your mind. Maybe you, yourself, have said or done something you wish you hadn't, but you think it's too late now to take it back. Whatever the problem is, the bottom line is that you are getting in your own way. You're letting negative energy rule your thoughts and behaviors.

Counsel

Get out of your own way. Stop sabotaging yourself. No matter what has happened or what was said, there is always another way to look at the situation. Forgive yourself and others when you're able to. We're all here to learn. There's always another day to start with a fresh slate and learn better ways to handle things. Learn from your mistakes, instead of harboring negative thoughts that just eat away at you and destroy your present moment, and then try your best not to make those mistakes again.

SPADE
EPEES

8

SWORDS
ESPADAS

SCHWERTER

ZWAARDEN

Key Words
Holding self back from dealing with
conflicts. Temporary difficulties.
Phobias

Eight of Swords

Consciousness

Some kind of fear, phobia, difficulty in coping with some problem or temporary illness, is making you feel as if you're trapped and can't move forward. You're allowing your fears to stand in your way. You have become a prisoner of your own mind. You may not be able to see it now, but you need to stop these debilitating thoughts from running in your mind. Ask them what they wish to teach you about yourself. What do you need to learn? What roots do you need to pull out from your garden?

Counsel

You need to develop a coping mechanism to get unstuck. Nothing is really holding you back but your own uncertainty and fears. Don't let your fears frighten you. See them as the opposing team in the sport of life, and challenge them. There are many sources for help at your disposal. Positive affirmation, prayer, energy healing and meditation are some suggestions. Call upon God and your spirit guides to help you remove what is blocking you from moving forward in life.

Key Words
Tension, anxieties, headaches,
sleeplessness, self pity

Nine of Swords

Consciousness

Stress and negative thinking have gotten way out of hand. Now you are not only dealing with anxiety, but headaches and insomnia, to boot. You have come down with a bad case of the "Poor Me" Disease. And of course, what does that attract back to you? More of the same, because that is the frequency you are vibrating at, and the channel you are tuned into watching on the screen of your worldly experiences. Whatever you're focusing on is bringing more of the same back to you, till you literally get sick of it and need help.

Counsel

Stress, headaches and insomnia could be effecting you. You need to feel some compassion for yourself, till you can get a grip on the reality you've gotten yourself into. It's OK to feel sorry for yourself for a little while. But don't stay at the the "Pity Party" too long, or you may end up being a repeated guest, and then have to deal with the next cycle's arrival of more of the same. You need to be in the vibrational frequency of what you want in order to get it. Is this what you want in your life? Be like a child and use your imagination to create a better reality in your head, with the pretend game, till what you desire takes form. Whatever it takes to do a 180 degree turn around to a better mind set, push yourself there, no matter how awful you feel at first. You are not alone. Pray, and call upon your spirit guides for help. They can not intervene unless you ask for their help. Eventually things will change.

| SPADE EPEES | 10 | SWORDS ESPADAS |
| SCHWERTER | | ZWAARDEN |

Key Words

Problems ending,exhaustion,

Ten of Swords

Consciousness

Don't let someone or something kill your hopes and dreams by giving them all your power. Perhaps someone in your childhood you depended on for love, hurt you to the core of your being. At the time it seemed like the only place to go was out, as in "Out of Your Body"....leaving only a tiny pilot light of present energy left for you to live with. You then grew up, still carrying the same baggage, never knowing how to reignite your fire. The world became a scary place to you, because you never learned how to stop being a magnet for that initial pain. The time has come for you to release any pain producing thoughts and let them go. Ask yourself what problem thinking is holding you back from the life you want to live. You may have reached rock bottom, or be too exhausted right now to deal with the situation, but whatever the problem was, seems to be leaving very soon.

Counsel

The world is not a scary place, but unhealed wounds, leaving your emotional body scarred, can cause you to feel like it is, when something happens and triggers your pain to the surface. The universe is going to continually send you stuff to bring back those old pains, so you can heal yourself. The perceptions you formed as a child don't have any power over you, unless you agree to let them. It's time to get off "The Martyr Train" and get on "The Soul Empowerment Train". You may feel totally drained or unable to function at the moment from whatever is going on. You need to take care of yourself and get help. An energy healer could be helpful. Take your power back. Extreme exhaustion could be lifting soon from a problem coming to an end very shortly.

FANTE DI SPADE   KNAVE OF SWORDS
VALET D'EPEES   SOTA DE ESPADAS

BUBE DER SCHWERTER   ZWAARDEN SCHILDKNAAP

Key Words
Defensive, protective
Baby, Young Child , Girl.

Page of Swords

Consciousness

Being a G.I.T. (God In Training) requires a lot of life experiences, to get the hang of it. One thing you need to learn is how to defend yourself with all different kinds of folks out there in the world. You have to know who you truly are to have a lot of self confidence. Knowing your True Self gives you the wisdom of diplomacy and soul maturity, so you won't want to cut off people's heads, when they judge you or put you down. If they knew better they would do better.

Counsel

Defend yourself. It's important to develop the kind of self confidence that comes from learning who you are. Accept and love yourself, just as you are, with all the various character traits that came with your packaging when you were born. Don't let anyone bully you around or mistreat you. But don't go overboard and become a control freak either. Remember you're a G.I.T. (a God In Training). It's good to stand up for something you believe in. Be careful not to go overboard and alienate your fellow planeteers, with such a defensive attitude that it makes your energy unapproachable. They will back off from you and find others more comfortable to be around, if you're too defensive.

Key Words
Impulsive, aggressive.
Slow down. Going too fast
Young Man

Knight of Swords

Consciousness

Nobody likes a bully or control freak. The Knight of Swords represents an impulsive, aggressive kind of energy towards people and life. Maybe you had a tough childhood, or kids in school picked on you, or weren't very nice to you, which you resented. You must learn to overcome these things, tame your animal nature and mature spiritually, so you don't take your repressed anger out onto others in the world. You need to slow down outwardly and grow up internally. At this level you may not be able to see that yet, and because of it, you may be way too impulsive and impatient with others (including yourself), in the situations presented to you.

Counsel

You need to slow down and know that you're not going to get your needs met by mowing down or intimidating people. Overly defensive mannerisms and aggressive behavior doesn't work and only causes negative consequences. It's a sure way for you to lose friends and end up being alone in the end, when people have had enough. You need to cool your jets, calm down, do some self reflective work, and weed out where this behavior originated from. Are you left feeling inner peace and happiness with your actions? This kind of attitude in life is only going to alienate you from others, plus you will need to be accountable for it at some time down the road. Think about the consequences of your actions before you act impulsively.

Key Words
Bossy, controlling, insensitive.
Defensive thinking.
Woman

171

Queen of Swords

Consciousness

You're not the touchy, feely, mushy type. You want something done right, and done right now. You may be accomplished in a worldly, material way, but sensitivity is not your strength. You don't want explanations or excuses. You want complete control of an outcome and you demand that it be done, no matter what. You can be rather self centered, bossy and defensive. You don't want your authority challenged either. Maybe you feel you've had it really rough in your climb up to the top. Perhaps you had to work really hard on your own. Doesn't matter. You don't feel like using your precious time for explanations to anyone, to justify yourself. You need to learn to be more compassionate and less self centered.

Counsel

Your intelligence and reliability enables you to analyze things quickly and get things done, which has shown you can be a valuable asset. The problem is that you lack sensitivity to others and tend to be a bit self centered. In delegating your authority, you can be a bit bossy and controlling at times, which you may not see, causing others to be somewhat offended and uncomfortable around you. You have to learn to be more compassionate and empathetic of others or they will get turned off by you, regardless of your other assets. Work on opening your heart.

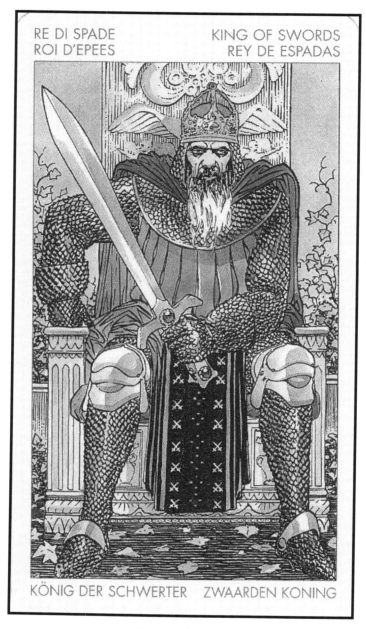

RE DI SPADE
ROI D'EPEES
KING OF SWORDS
REY DE ESPADAS

KÖNIG DER SCHWERTER   ZWAARDEN KONING

Key Words
Very controlling, tyrant.
Stubbornly defensive.
Cold blooded insensitivity. Man

King of Swords

Consciousness

The King of Swords is all about ego, arrogance, and manipulation. Being at this level, you can be rather self centered, insensitive and intimidating to others. You see other people's sensitivities as weaknesses to take advantage of, and make your own sensitivities more important than theirs. You'd rather be in control and have people be afraid of you, then let them see your own insecurities. Your intelligence and troubleshooting abilities to get things done can be a great asset, however you tend to huff and puff and blow other people's self esteem down, to build up your own, whether you're conscious or not that you are doing this.

Counsel

While you can be very intelligent and sort through problems with quick resolutions, you must learn to be more considerate of other's needs and sensitivities. Soften your approach to others and you will get more accomplished, by building better relationships both now and down the road. Try not to harp on the problems in life. Focus your keen mind on what can be done to improve things in the world, and be more positive in your outlook. Learn to see the good in others, instead of their faults. Whatever you look for you will find more of.

DENARI
DENIERS

1

PENTACLES
OROS

MÜNZEN

MUNTEN

Key Words
New money or material things.
Winter

Ace of Pentacles

Consciousness

Your attention is now focused on money and material things. This is the time to make an intention of precisely what you want, and visualize it's manifestation. Energy follows thought, so know what you want and what you want it for. You are a sending and receiving station, so pay attention to what your thoughts are broadcasting out into the ethers. Whatever channel you are tuned into is going to be doing the attracting. Are you focusing on abundance or not having enough (lack consciousness)? The supply of whatever you want is unlimited, if you believe it is. The opposite is also true. So think positive and believe! Now is a good time to manifest abundance.

Counsel

New opportunities in money and material things are heading your way. Think big. Nothing is too much in a world of limitless abundance. Whatever your mind can believe, you can conceive. Allowing your good in takes practice, and there is no better time then right now to start training your brain to believe in possibility thinking. Put out an intention for what you want and focus your attention on that, not what you don't want. Plant seeds of prosperity consciousness in the garden of your mind. Using prosperity affirmations and creating vision boards of things you want to manifest can be very helpful.

Key Words
Balancing money and material
aspects of life

Two of Pentacles

Consciousness

Decisions, decisions, decisions. Back and forth you are juggling your time, options, choices, moods and actions. You've got x amount of time and money to do such and such by such and such. What should you do? You're going back and forth, without the exact results you are seeking yet. You are on a tipping scale here, of whether to believe or not in possibilities. Will you go with the comfort of your old lack consciousness way of thinking or shift to creating a prosperity consciousness that allows unlimited possibilities. This card indicates a need for balancing your energy and weighing the pros and cons of a situation, and what to do about it.

Counsel

You may be doing a juggling act here, trying to keep things and thoughts in balance. Try not to stay on the fence too long, making decisions. No choice is still a choice. Ask your guides to help you every day, whatever way you need help, and then be open to what inspirations come to your mind. Be observant in the world of form, remembering it's your consciousness that is the creator of what forms in your reality. What you are viewing and experiencing (what's on your radar) has already been set in motion by previous thoughts put into actions. What choices you make today will effect tomorrow's experiences.

Key Words
Recognition, responsibility
and validation

Three of Pentacles

Consciousness

You are learning the value of being recognized for your efforts and creations. The most important person you want to impress is yourself, for that is where your self worth originates from. Whatever you do in life stems from the beliefs you established about yourself along life's journey. Were you recognized by your parents, teachers and peers in your earlier years? How did this make you feel about yourself? Did you gain or lose self confidence by their words and actions towards you? Are there any negative feelings still lingering in your subconscious that are holding you back, causing you to continue to attract more of the same experiences? If so, make an effort to root out these negative weeds in your mind, so you can heal and create a better future for yourself. Did you receive praise, that helped you to achieve in life? If so, where can you offer praise and support to someone else who may not have had such an advantage in their life's journey?

Counsel

Something is coming up that will give you an opportunity to feel praised, validated or recognized. It could be a meeting, an interview, a performance, or something more personal. Do your best, achieve what you can and feel proud of yourself, even if it's just overcoming a hardship or learning something new. When you feel good about yourself, others take notice and you attract, by your vibration, further recognition from others. If you find yourself having trouble achieving in life, look to see where you may need to work on self validation. The starting point for validation always begins from within. Take one step at a time at whatever level you can handle.

Key Words
Security issues with
hanging on or letting go

Four of Pentacles

Consciousness

What are you still holding onto that's getting in the way of living the life you want? Who or what is it that you can't seem to let go of? What memories have become so ingrained in your subconscious that they are sabotaging your ability to move forward? Is it a grudge? If so, the only one you're hurting is yourself. Is it the love you lost, the love you never had, a betrayal of trust or abandonment? Whatever it is let it go. Don't let these thoughts and memories ruin another moment of your life force. Put your trust in God, that things happen for reasons you don't always understand, and may never understand (at least not until you return to your celestial home). Look at life as a series of lessons. You must work on your vibration and fine tune your frequency to attract what you want. To make space for new opportunities to come in, you have to let go of the old.

Counsel

Holding onto the past just ruins the present, and attracts more of whatever you're holding onto, because you're still resonating at the same frequency. Work on your vibration at the earliest sign of a problem. Release whatever it is that you may still be holding onto and free up your energy to create better in the next cycle. Learn to detach from the illusions of the material plane, and remember it is you that is creating your reality. You might be holding onto things, people or memories you don't need anymore, to feel secure. Make space for the new to come in.

Key Words
Out in the cold.
Consciousness of lack

Five of Pentacles

Consciousness

With the Five of Pentacles, you are functioning at a vibration of lack consciousness. You can't trust or believe that something better could possibly be available to you, so you settle for less. You feel unworthy of abundance or anything good happening for you. You haven't let go of a belief that has lodged itself in your subconscious memory, causing you to feel this way. The more you focus on lack, the more you are perpetuating lack to radiate into your energy field. You must change the vibration you are tuned into, in order for the universe to provide you with the abundance and good health you truly deserve.

Counsel

Block out those negative thoughts that are causing you to remain at "The Poor Me Party." If you aren't ready to leave there yet, at least love yourself for where you are, and grow where you're planted. Start a new habit of prosperity and love consciousness thinking, with the help of positive affirmations or self hypnosis tapes to help diminish those old tapes, still playing in your head. Repeat them over and over, till it becomes who you are in energy, and you actually start believing it. The results will start showing up if you practice with persistence. Pray for the help you need, and trust that your guides are there for you to call upon. You are good enough and you deserve abundance in all areas of your life. Believe in yourself! Love yourself! As your beliefs change, so will your experiences.

Key Words
Putting out to get back.
Karmic justice

Six of Pentacles

Consciousness

At the Six of Pentacles you're beginning to understand what it means to live in a vibrational world of cause and effect. By shifting your vibrational frequency, new energy patterns are emerging and taking form in your reality. You are non physical energy, living in the vessel of a physical body, giving shape and form to the energy of matter, through the filtered direction of your mind's commands. When you truly know this, through experienced learning, you will then have the desire to get your energy moving in the direction of that which you wish to experience. You will then no longer choose to blame others for your experiences. This is actually a good thing, because it takes you out of victim thinking, and gives you your power back, as a creator. The energy of your beliefs, combined with your karmic debts and credits, are the magnets of your attracted experiences. "As you sow, so shall you reap". There is a divine order in the world. Whatever good or bad energy you have been putting out into the world is coming back to you now.

Counsel

Be mindful of what you are sowing, for "As you sow, so shall you reap". Everything is energy - thoughts, words, actions, things....even you! What you are experiencing right now is the result of the energy you have already put out into the world. Do good things and send out positive loving energy to yourself and others, and that's what you can expect to come back to you. The opposite is also true. What goes ' round, comes ' round. Make a difference in someone else's life and someone will make a difference in yours. Love yourself and you will attract the love of others.

DENARI 7 PENTACLES
DENIERS OROS

MÜNZEN MUNTEN

Key Words
Work is almost done. Evaluating
investment

Seven of Pentacles

Consciousness

With the Seven of Pentacles, you are taking an overview of your current efforts and experiences. Do you like what you see? Are you getting satisfactory results to what you have given your time, money and life energy to? What is your heart telling you? What is your bank account telling you? To invest or not to invest any further in this direction or path? That is the question....be it a job, a project, a financial matter, a relationship or a partnership. Everything in front of you is a mirror of what you have caused into being. What areas do you need more work in? Is it worth the effort? Here you are sending out vibrations of uncertainty as to whether things will improve or not in the direction you're moving. Now is the time to accept what you can not change and make the decision to change what you can, going forward.

Counsel

Look at the choices you have made up till this point, before planting the seeds of new choices. Time to take personal inventory in yourself, with where you are now vs. where you would like to be in the future. If you stay where you are, will it be worth the life energy you'll be investing in it, or are there other areas of your life you would rather devote your energy to right now? Are you happy with the life you have created up to this point? If not, make a decision to make changes where you can, and accept what can no longer be changed. Trust that you have done the best you could with what you knew at each moment. Don't waste the vital time you have left lamenting over what can no longer be changed. See each experience you have had as part of your soul's education.

Key Words
Working steadily on a project or
beginning a new one

Eight of Pentacles

Consciousness

The Eight of Pentacles is all about staying committed to the things you desire, and giving them your full attention, energy and action, till you get the results you want. Here you are doing what you enjoy doing and working towards a goal you wish to achieve with it. You are in the zone now, flowing downstream, with what feels natural to your soul's right path and purpose. A sense of mission fuels your passions. You are developing yourself further, improving your skills and talents, becoming more of who you are, and feeling more alive in the process.

Counsel

You're passions are igniting your soul with joy now. Keep moving in the direction you're going, developing your skills and talents, working on yourself and becoming a master of "YOU, Incorporated". The only one you need to compete with is yourself and what's going to make your life feel more fulfilled and fun for you. Do what you love, do your best and don't worry about what others think. Listen to the song of your own soul. You are unique and there are things that only you can bring to the world. Doors of opportunity are opening up to you because of your level of attraction, magnetizing them to you. The feeling of being "alive" is in the journey of discovering the puzzle pieces of your life that make you feel more of who you are. Here the enjoyment of your work is helping you discover some of those puzzle pieces.

DENARI 9 PENTACLES
DENIERS OROS

MÜNZEN MUNTEN

Key Words
Peace of mind
from accomplishment

Nine of Pentacles

Consciousness

At the Nine of Pentacles you feel a peace of mind, and inner joy that comes from seeing the rewards of your accomplishments. You can now take a moment to relax and enjoy the fruits of your labor. By believing in yourself and following your heart, you have manifested your dreams. Coming to this point has given you a deep feeling of connection with the world around you. You radiate a glow of contentment, that draws the attention of others to you. There is a deep sense of satisfaction in the freedom of independence and self reliance you have developed at this stage, yet the love and light filled joy you feel, gives you the desire to share your energy with others. There is nothing like " feeling good" to attract and create more of the same.

Counsel

It's time to enjoy the rewards of your accomplishments. Take time to relax now and appreciate how far you've come. Because your light is glowing, people are drawn to you and want to be in your energy field. By keeping your peaceful state of mind going, no matter what is happening around you, things will continue to go well for you. You are in the vortex. Even if you should stray from this state of mind, it will be easier now to know how to get back in it.

Key Words
Material success.
Potential expansions

Ten of Pentacles

Consciousness

The Ten of Pentacles is all about accomplishment and expansion. Life is a place to grow your soul and learn from the expansion of your own creations. Even after you have graduated from one school of learning in life there is always another classroom waiting to be filled along your journey, to higher levels in the ladder of evolution. The more you create, the more you learn about who you are and your potential. Whatever is in front of you right now is what you have attracted into your field of energy, due to the concentrated efforts of your focused thought and actions. Much like television, there are many shows and commercials going on in life simultaneously. What channel are you currently viewing and tuned into? Are you happy with the show you're watching? What improvements and expansions can you bring to the table for yourself and others to benefit from, with the wisdom you've acquired?

Counsel

Allow yourself to feel good about the life you have manifested. You are unique. Whatever you've created was tailor made for whatever you needed to learn from. What new horizons do you still wish to create for yourself and the world? What would you like to leave as your legacy? What would you like to do differently now? This is the time for expansions and transitions. Your emotions are the barometer of whether you've been successfully on track with your life or where you need to expand in new directions.

FANTE DI DENARI   KNAVE OF PENTACLES
VALET DE DENIERS   SOTA DE OROS

BUBE DER MÜNZEN   MUNTEN SCHILDKNAAP

Key Words

Totally absorbed in something.
Student. Message about
money or material thing.
Baby, young child, girl

Page of Pentacles

Consciousness

Something or someone has captivated your interest, that you want to give most, if not all of your attention to. You're consumed with whomever or whatever it is, sometimes to the exclusion of all else. This is all you want to focus on for now, so you can give it your all. You want to take time to study something or someone you want to learn more about. There is a tendency, at this stage, of getting so absorbed in whatever has captured your interest, that other things fall out of balance. Keep your eye on the goal, but be alert to your surroundings as well. The time may also be ripe for understanding and learning a lesson, or taking a class in something you would like to study.

Counsel

Now is the time for concentration, study and practiced action. If you want to really learn, accomplish or perfect anything, this is what you need to do. Observe and study whatever message, situation or emotion is coming to you in the moment, because it is coming into your energy field for a reason. It could very well be a lesson or message in need of your immediate attention, while still on your radar. Juice the moment and take the time right now to figure out what it's trying to tell you. If something you would enjoy studying has captured your interest, now would be a good time to enroll in a class.

CAVALLO DI DENARI   KNIGHT OF PENTACLES
CHEVALIER DE DENIERS   CABALLO DE OROS

RITTER DER MÜNZEN   MUNTEN RIDDER

Key Words
Surveying where you wish to go.
Creating a vision for action.
Young man

Knight of Pentacles

Consciousness

Here you are taking an overview of the bigger picture of an idea that has ignited your interest, and surveying where you could potentially go with it. Sparks of possibilities are flying around in your mind. You see something in need of change or improvement that you would like to put into action, and you believe you have what it takes to make it happen. Your idea is building into a vision. A passionate desire, motivated by a sense of purpose, is fueling your imagination, for turning this idea into a reality. There is a deep feeling building in you, which is leading you to believe you can really make a difference with this idea. This vision of yours could very well become a mission for you.

Counsel

A sense of purpose is motivating you to put an idea into action. You need to focus your mind and get a clear mental image of how you would like to see this idea take form. By holding a vision for your idea, you are building an energy vortex, a virtual blueprint, for turning your dream into a reality. The rockets of desire you are sending out into the universe are propelled by the intensity of your enthusiasm. This is creating a powerful level of magnetic attraction for manifesting the ways to make this happen for you.

REGINA DI DENARI   QUEEN OF PENTACLES
REINE DE DENIERS   REINA DE OROS

KÖNIGIN DER MÜNZEN   MUNTEN KONINGIN

Key Words
Conscious awareness of
Strengths and weaknesses. Woman

Queen of Pentacles

Consciousness

The Queen of Pentacles has you reflecting on the journey of your life, what you have learned about who you are and what you have done with the talents and traits you have been given. What have you discovered about yourself - your strengths and weaknesses? If you were to create a brand of yourself what would it be about? How would you describe the brand of you to someone else? It's time to take stock in the person you have created, see what it is about you that sets you apart from others, and makes you unique. At this stage of your journey, you must come to love and accept yourself, just as you are, with all your talents, traits and flaws. See the good you have done for the world and how you have helped the lives of others, besides your own. It's a good time to think of how you would like to be remembered by others and what impact you have had, or would still like to make on the lives of others.

Counsel

It's time for you to take personal inventory of your strengths and weaknesses. Invest in yourself. It's not about what they see. It's about what you see when you look into that mirror. Focus on the positive things that you have done and things you want to work on. Get a clear picture of how you can use time to your best advantage, to feel good about yourself. Above all be positive. You probably need to give yourself a lot more credit then you have been doing for making a difference in the lives of many, including your own. Chalk up what doesn't please you, as lessons you have learned from, and accept yourself as you are. You need to love and appreciate yourself and the journey you have chosen for your life.

RE DI DENARI · KING OF PENTACLES
ROI DE DENIERS · REY DE OROS

KÖNIG DER MÜNZEN · MUNTEN KONING

Key Words
Material Accomplishment. Wealth. Man

King of Pentacles

Consciousness

Having learned about yourself, by going inward at the Queen of Pentacles, you now want to project outward at the King of Pentacles. What can you do to help others and give back from the good fortune you have achieved in life? What have you learned and acquired in life that could be of benefit to help others, who may not have had the same opportunities as you? What talents, acquisitions and traits do you have, that you can use to help make the world a better place to live in? Where can you support someone else's growth with what you've learned in life, or help others in need? What legacy do you want to be remembered for, that will leave the world a better place, both now and after you have gone?

Counsel

Time to not only enjoy what you have achieved in life, but also to give back, invest in others, work on spiritual development, go green or take up some worthy cause to help the world. You'll feel better on the inside, and not just from trying to impress others with what you've got and who you are, materially. Be more open to how you can be of service to others. Show kindness and compassion to others less fortunate or different than yourself. You'll be amazed at what it does for your energy of attraction. People will begin to like you for who you are and not just what you have.

Tarot Spreads and Sample Reading

Tarot Card Spreads

1. Yes or No Spread
(For questions that can be answered with a Yes or No)

2. Question and Answer Spread
(For quick answers to general questions)

3. Celtic Block Spread
(For general readings or overview of an area of concern)

4. The Higher and Lower Pyramid Spread
(How to use the whole deck for longer readings)

5. Yearly Forecast Spread
(For Month to Month Readings)

****
Reader always shuffles the deck first with intention of clearing it

Before each spread, client shuffles the deck while question or subject of concern is being thought of (unless it's a general reading). Then client cuts the deck in 3 piles and puts the deck back into one pile, in the way of their choice, before handing it back to reader.

The cards are then placed right side up, into position of spread being read, except for spreads 2. and 5., which are placed right side up after being placed in position of spread.

For comparing options use spread 3. and pick 3 cards for each option being considered, even if one of the options is unknown. Use last 3 cards to answer possibility of unknown option.

1. Yes or No Spread

(For Questions that can be answered with a Yes or No)

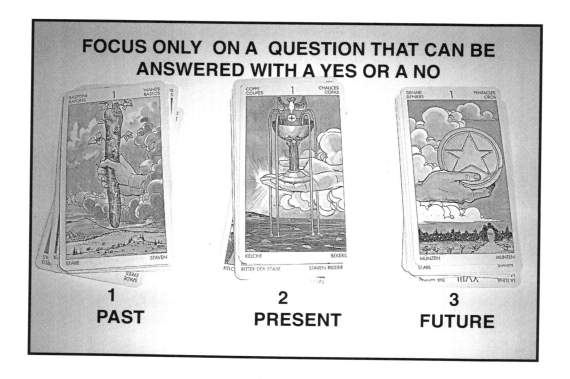

FOCUS ONLY ON A QUESTION THAT CAN BE ANSWERED WITH A YES OR A NO

1
PAST

2
PRESENT

3
FUTURE

Client should focus on question, shuffle the question into the deck, divide the deck into 3 piles and then put back into one pile, whatever way is desired. Then hand back to the reader. The reader then turns up 13 cards from the top of the deck to create first pile unless an ace shows up. Even if the ace is the first card stop and go onto second pile. Repeat this till you have 3 piles. The more aces you have the more likely the answer is a yes. The less aces the more likely the answer is a no. Use the bottom card of the remaining deck for further information. The bottom card in each pile can also be used for further information. Cards other than aces are past, present and future influences for further information.

2. Question and Answer Spread
(For quick answers to general questions)

FAN CARDS OUT IN SEMI CIRCLE

PAST	PRESENT	FUTURE
1	2	3

Reader fans out cards. Client focuses mind on question, scans left hand over cards and chooses 3 cards, given over to reader in sequence as picked. They are then placed face down. Reader then turns them right side up in order gotten, before reading them.

3. Celtic Block Spread
(For general readings or overview of an area of concern)

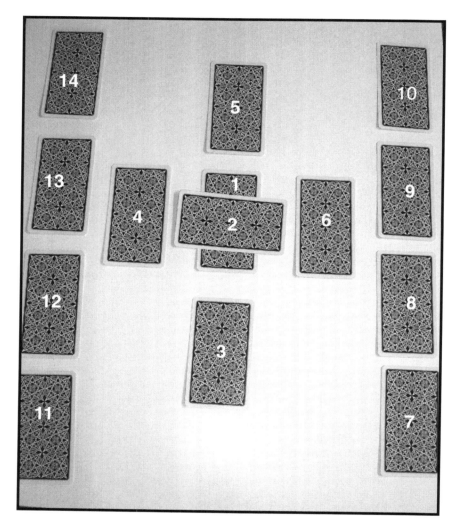

1 - Current Situation
2 - What is Influencing it
3 - Foundation
4 - The Past
5 - What's on MInd
6 - Near Future
7 - Fears, Concerns
8 - Current Environment
9 - Wishes, Desires

10 - Outcome 8-9 *
11 - Physical World
12 - Emotional World
13 - Mental World
14 - Spiritual World

* 8-9 days, weeks, months,
   or 8th or 9th month

4. The Higher and Lower Pyramid Spread
How to use the whole deck for longer readings

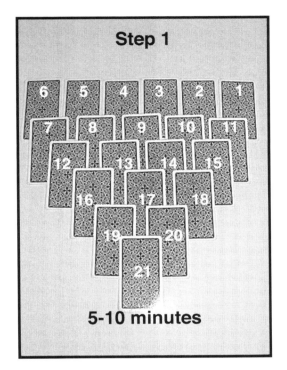

Step 1

5-10 minutes

Step 2

15 -20 minutes

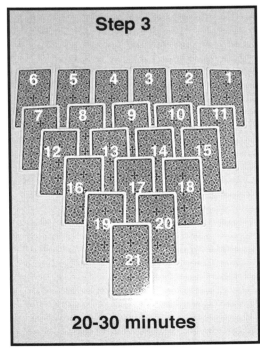

Step 3

20-30 minutes

5. Yearly Forecast Spread
(For Month to Month Readings)

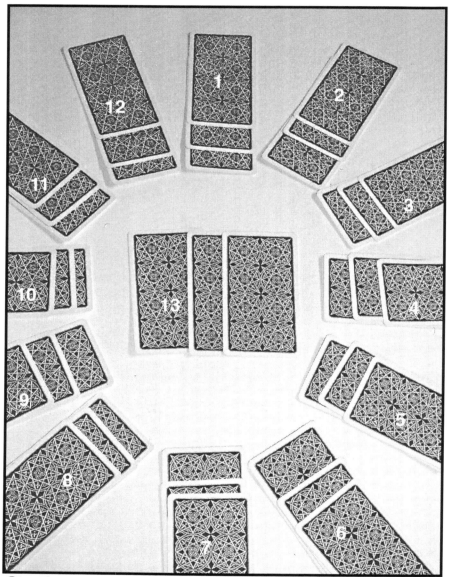

Starting at position of card #1 (January) lay out cards going clock work in a circle. When you get to #12 (December) put a card in the middle and then repeat 3 times as shown. The Middle cards are a summary of the year. Read each month (1-12) like Spread #3. Same for Middle cards. (Read 1st)

Sample Reading

(Transcribed from an actual tape recorded reading with a client, and performed with the understanding that this reading would be used as a teaching demonstration. The client, in this case, would be the student model chosen for our Tarot Classroom in the book.)

Starting with the Celtic Block Spread
(We are now at the beginning of our 1/2 hour tarot card reading)

For the purpose of privacy to the client, he will from this point on in the reading be known as Merlin. In real life, he is an astrologer and a fine artist, with an upcoming art show he is concerned about.

The client is shuffling the deck, dividing it into three piles and putting it back into one pile. Now I am laying them out. I am using the Universal Tarot by Lo Scarabeo. Refer to the Sample Reading photos as you read here.

The cards that are showing up right now are the **8 of pentacles** (1-current situation), **The Queen of Wands** (2-influencing), **The Emperor** (4-recent past), **The King of Pentacles** (5-mind), **The World** card (6-near future), and **The Knight of Swords** (is in the 7-fears department). **The nine of pentacles** (is in 8-current environment), **The High Priestess** (is in the 9-wish area), and you've got **The Ten of Wands** (10-outcome). **The Hierophant** is on the left column (11-physical world), above that is **The Knight of Pentacles** (12 - emotional world), above that is **The Tower** (13-mental world) and **The Seven of Wands** (14-spiritual world area).

On the left column- These are the four worlds of existence - the physical world, emotional world, mental world and spiritual world. A **lot of times in the spiritual world area, your spirit guides will show up.** What comes up in the spread areas of the Mental World, What's on your Mind (the upper card in the middle column), and the Wishes Area (the right column) - will show you what you are attracting to yourself, what your mind is magnetically generating back to you.

What they're saying right now is, that you need to be more patient with getting what you want, because **The World** card is in the Near Future Area of the cross. That's saying that you have every ability of getting what you want, that you are to learn something from it now, and you will learn it.

The High Priestess is telling you that you what you desire is going through a period of gestation and development. You need to listen to your intuition and guidance from within, to know, with out doubt, that it's going to happen. She has a choice. Is she going to think positive or negative? The two polls next to her represent positive and negative thinking, the white is positive and the black is negative. The black column also represents her subconscious mind and the white column, her conscious mind.

What's going on behind that curtain? What is lying behind that curtain are the fruits of her subconscious thoughts, represented by those pomegranates. What they are saying to you is, whose that man behind that curtain? ....like it's said in The Wizard of Oz. (We all hide behind the curtain of of our personas). Like you, the Wizard, is just a person, but that person, is hiding what's going on within, subconsciously.

The High Priestess is you. Your subconscious thoughts are the stuff that's growing behind the curtain, and the message here, is what are the fruits you are allowing, subconsciously, to grow in the garden of your mind, right now? The crescent moon, on the bottom of the card, is saying that your emotions are playing an important role in your thinking too. Are you going to allow your emotions to be used for spiritual development, or let them hold you back, with doubt?

Your subconscious thoughts do a lot of creating. If you don't know what's going on there, you could be creating unconsciously, from your subconscious thoughts. It looks to me (if I look at the card in the Mental Area of the spread), that you are carrying outworn belief systems you need to weed out, that are subconsciously causing your experiences to fall apart.

The **Seven of Wands** in the Spiritual Area, **is saying you need to get rid of self doubt, and that you can handle whatever comes your way.** All those wands coming at you are saying, I need to battle my way through the world, I need to deal with this one, with that one, and I don't like this one's personality. This one is giving me a hard time, or that art show is supposed to be a certain way. So it's saying your lesson, **your spiritual lesson** (because this card is in the spiritual world area of the spread), **is to get rid of the self doubts......Be like your Creator,.......be like God.......be the God in Training that you are. Don't doubt that you are the creator of your experience. Know that you are the creator of your reality and can create whatever you want, positively or don't want, negatively.**

The Hierophant, on the first rung of the left column of the spread, is saying, you have teachers in the world who can help you and guide you, but use your own intuition. Be the teacher to yourself - observe your life, and be the authority of your own experiences.

Next, let's look at **The Tower**, in The Mental World Area. Ask yourself what thoughts do you need to weed out from your subconscious, that are no longer serving you.

The **High Priestess**, from the white, conscious mind column of the card, is saying, I want this, but the black, subconscious mind column, is saying, I've got all this stuff from my past, getting in my way. The Past Area of the spread, represented by **The Emperor** is saying, I've been rigid. Things have to be a certain way and at a certain time.

The **Nine of Pentacles** (in the Current Environment Area) says, I want to be at peace with myself, and I want money for my accomplishments. I have established myself with the **Four of Wands** (1- foundation card) and I want to see some results with that **World** card (6- near future).

The Universe is saying, be patient, what you want is in a state of development, with **The High Priestess** being in the Wish Area. You're in the incubator stage. The **Ten of Wands,** in the Outcome Area - 10) is saying take the burden off yourself. Stop pressuring yourself.

Move your hand further away from your face, so you can see past your burdens, and then take a look at your situation, so you can see what you've actually created. Then stop putting all these burdens on yourself (**Ten of Wands),** like your success has to rigidly arrive at a certain time and place, like **The Emperor** says. the **Knight of Pentacles** (at the Emotional World Area) is giving his own opinion, by saying, looking over your life, you've gone through quite a bit, however, you've built up a lot of positive experiences and you have the talent to achieve your goal. Maybe you've needed to take time to really observe every little angle of your life, so that you can be a real expert - not just at your art and your astrology, but so you can be an expert at life. Then the **Knight of Pentacles** is saying with his armor (defenses) and his Black horse (the darkness of his subconscious), I'm looking at where I want to be at a certain time and place in life, and I want to be making a certain amount of money. I have all this fire in my mind. (See all the fire coming out of the helmet's back. The colors of the feathers even look like fire). He has all this armor (strong protective defenses), that make it hard for him to penetrate his deeper self, **so he has to learn how he can use his subconscious to move himself forward in life, instead of thinking about how to protect himself from it.** That's how you deal with emotions, and why he is in the emotional area, to talk to you.

The Hierophant, (as the teacher) is saying, **Okay, there's a whole lot of knowledge and wisdom out there** (symbolized by the keys on the card), **that people are going to want to counsel you with, or tell you what to do what with what. But everyone is coming from their own point of view, and most people are going to tell you stuff, according to what's going to validate what they want. They may not validate what you want. So be the teacher to yourself. Be a conscious observer of what you want, and don't look for validation on the outside, except for what you want to create for yourself.**

If it's money you want, do it for you. Don't do it because you want to get validation. You'll get the validation no matter what, if you believe in yourself, and get rid of self-doubt. The Seven of Wands is saying, That's what you need to work on. And then you have the **Nine of Swords** (in the Fear Area) whose saying, **there is a desire to do things impulsively, when it comes to things you're afraid of. You think to**

yourself, life is not exactly slowing up and so I need to speed things up. I'm speeding things up because I'm afraid. I don't want to leave this life without having my wants and dreams manifested. But they are saying the way to go is not to speed things up, but rather slow down and go inward. Find out what your subconscious is broadcasting, that you may not be aware is creating your reality, without your conscious awareness.

King of Pentacles (in the Mind Area), says to you, you've got the talent and experience, so where's my stuff? I've got the talent, I'm doing the work, so where's my stuff - the money, the wealthy lifestyle? I want it, and I want it now, not ten or more years later. The High Priestess then says, You've got the goods, but you're not pushing your talents ahead with the right thoughts and attitudes. Are you really believing in yourself and your talents, as you claim you do?

The Tower, then answers, well here's your lesson, Merlin. Break away from those old patterns you used to think - that the world is such a scary place, that you have to put on your armor to deal with it (the Knight of Pentacles).

Be your own teacher, observe your own validating - or non validating thoughts that you're telling yourself and get rid of self-doubt. Don't be so rigid like The Emperor, that things have to be in a certain way or happen in a certain time. Even the Queen of Wands is saying don't let your subconscious emotions get in your way. Look at your skills, with your emotions and subconscious out of the way, by learning from them. Listen to their voice.

From what we've learned so far, the primary thing you need to work on, at this time, is giving more attention to the hidden lessons you have been missing, in order to succeed both spiritually and materially with your work.

(We are now continuing onto the next level of the layout using the Higher and Lower Pyramid directly over the Celtic Block, till the the whole deck is used)

The Higher and Lower Pyramid
(Beginning from the right to the left, going down first)

The Pyramid - Down

Now we've come to the next rung of the ladder in this reading. We are going into the higher and lower pyramid section, with the first pyramid going down. The first card we come to on the upper right corner is the **Page of Swords,** where you're beginning to see where you have been defensive, and how that defensiveness has really caused a burden for you, being next to the **Ten of Wands**. You've got the **Ten of Cups** card saying, you feel like you've been working diligently and want the reward of contentment from it. **The Ten of wands says,** that you've been working really hard. The **Six of Wands** is saying, I've done a good job, now where's my reward? The **Two of Swords** is saying, I can't deal with with something. The **Nine of Wands** then says, I've been through the mill. Then looking back at your life, the **Five of Cups,** says, you have to get rid of all the old regrets. Stop thinking about the past and how it was supposed to happen, or you will keep putting out the same vibration, which will cause you to just repeat more of the same stuff.

You wonder, where is that fancy estate, that fancy car, that money and whatever it is that you desire for the rewards for your work? (It doesn't have too be that. It could be whatever it is that you desire as rewards for your work. It could be anything.) The **Five of Cups** says, look at all those cups you still have left here. Take that dark cloak of negative thinking off yourself. You need to block out this negative energy you are currently vibrating at. Get into a positive vibration with an attitude of gratitude, and focus on what's going right.

Take into consideration what the **Seven of Wands** is saying. Get rid of the self doubt about how things are supposed to be. Trust that there is a reason for everything happening as it is. **The Fool** on the next rung of the ladder, down the pyramid, is telling you **it's not about the finish line. It's about the journey and your observations on the journey.**

Let your light shine. Be happy. Take that dark cloak off, Merlin. Keeping that black cloak on means you want to be invisible, and it's not working for you. Be courageous. The **Nine of Wands** then says, believe in yourself and put yourself out there, no matter what you have to deal with. Do it for the joy of doing it and not for the rewards. Eventually things will fall into place. The **Five of Wands** then says, I really want to believe, but I've got inner conflicts. Where do I put my energy? I'm going this way and that way. Scarecrow, which way do I go? You need to get focused.

Next the **Judgment** card is saying, get judgment out of the way. Being right next to **The High Priestess,** the message is still, it's going to happen when it happens. In the meantime, like the tower is telling you on the left, break down those old belief systems.

In the next row, t**he Nine of Swords** is saying, I am drained. I'm tired. The **Lovers card** is saying, bask in the love you have in your life. The communication that you have in your relationship life, your married life, and with your spirit guides and Angels is great. You work with them all very well, even in your work. But they're also saying, where is your communication and relationship with yourself? That's what's tiring you out, with the **Ten of Swords**.

The Queen of Cups says, you tend to worry a lot. You're looking into that magic mirror and saying, Mirror, mirror on the wall, who's the fairest of them all? and then saying to yourself, Well it ain't me. It's somebody else. I have all this talent. How come I'm not getting to be the fairest one. This sucks!

They're saying, stop worrying. **The Moon** is also saying, you worry too much. You have a fear of the unknown, causing you to worry. I want the bucks for my efforts. Where is it? The **Three of Wands** says, look at what you're projecting into your planning? **The Ten of Swords** then says, I'm including in my planning (not consciously of course) that I am also going to be friggin exhausted! (cause my inner pilot light won't be nourished enough to provide adequate positive attraction energy for myself)

I'm going to expose my art (my souls' innermost expression) and how are they going to review me? What the heck are they going say about me and my work? What if they don't make me famous? What if they

say my show sucks and blah, blah, blah......and what if, what if, what if? What if they cause me pain instead of pleasure ? (with **The Devil** and **Death** cards talking in your head)

So then the **Two of Pentacles** says, **Well Merlin, It's your choice. Are you going to let negative thinking get in your way? Are you going to let that inner Devil hold you hostage in your own head? Are you going to let your own ego's negativity hold you bondaged as a prisoner in your own mind?** The black color of the Devil's card represents mastery over the material world (like the martial artist's "black" belt), the dark world of negativity, and the dark inner world of the subconscious.

The Pyramid - Going Up

Now we're going back up the pyramid. I am looking at the **Page of Cups.** He is looking at the surprise phone calls and feelings coming in, and he is telling you, not knowing when certain feelings are going to come up can cause you to be impulsive (by his appearance next to **The Knight of Swords.)** In the row above him, the **Ace of Swords** wants him to take some action. He wants to make money and get recognition. That's what's motivating his action. The **Strength** card and the **Nine of Cups** in the row above that is saying, You need to be courageous in the pursuit of getting what you want. The **Ace of Wands says,** Allow new positive thoughts to create new ideas. **The Empress** is saying, you need to love yourself enough not to care about what others think. Stop feeling like you've got to put your armor on with the **Knight of Pentacles.** What if they don't love me? What if they think I'm this? What if they think I'm that? What if they don't like my work and don't want to buy it?

A fire is burning up in your subconscious mind and the cards are saying to get past that. The **Ace of Pentacles** says, there is money coming. Believe you can manifest. Use your subconscious to work with you. The card above you, **The Tower,** says to **break through those old patterns and outworn tapes, still keeping your subconscious under their hypnotic spell. Be kinder to yourself. Be a lover of you. Be a lover of everything you do - a lover of your thoughts, a lover of your process, even a lover of the fact that you judge yourself and say bad things to yourself**

sometimes. It's all part of your learning curve. Whatever it is, be a lover of the good stuff and the bad stuff, because it's all teaching you about who you are, through your journey.

The **Queen of Pentacles**, **Ten of Pentacles** and **Page of Pentacles** are saying, you're learning from money now. A lot of swords cards come after that, telling you about all the conflicts in your way, that you will need to overcome. But even conflict, if you learn to use it for bettering yourself along your journey, can be a really good thing. Only from having experienced the dark, can you really appreciate the light, so learn to see the light in all your experiences.

Look for the gifts in your adversities. The cards are telling you to change your perception. The **Queen of Pentacles** is asking you to look at both your abilities and limitations, and to ask yourself what you've learned in life from them. Her bare foot showing says, How can I risk letting the public see who I truly am, when I expose my art to the world? My truth, my soul and my art will all be exposed. Will I get the recognition I want, or will I be disappointed? Is the risk worth it?

With **The Hermit,** you're reflecting on yourself in the future, looking back into your current life, using your imagination to visualize it. You're going into your past and future to get a better perspective on the current life you wish to experience. **The Page of Pentacles** continues this study of yourself. In the future, in those older years of your life, is this where you want to be? Now take yourself back to the the present, and say to yourself, How do I get there? What do I need to learn?

The **Five of Pentacles** is saying, Though you might feel abandoned and all alone at times, there is always going to be someone there to help you, your spirit guide or some person sent to you by God. The creator will always send somebody to help you. God may be invisible, but the people he sends to help you are not, so you don't have to feel like you're abandoned and have to do everything on your own.

The **Six of Swords** let's you know that things should start getting better soon, showing smoother times lie ahead for you, as you move forward. **The Empress** reminds you to love yourself.

Next we see the **Five of Swords** and the **Eight of Swords.** What trips you up sometimes, is that you're afraid to take the next step. You hold yourself back with the "What if" disease. What if this happens? What if that happens? I can't do this. I can't do that. What if they crucify me? No one has crucified you, yet you are saying, but what if they do? With the **Five of Swords,** you're already projecting you're going to get pissed off and want to strangle them or kill them (not literally, of course) with the **Death** card. And so, this is you getting in your own way, with your own thoughts, as we see in the **Eight of Swords.** She can easily get out of those loose ropes if she wants to. There are no locks and those ropes are very loose.

The Star card is saying to come out of your shell. With the exposure of her naked self, her message is to expose your truth, your true Self. It's okay. The worst thing that can possibly happen is that you're right. Maybe, for some reason, there will be disappointment. Maybe there will be things you are not so crazy about. But so what? **The Judgement** card says, Why the heck should I care about what they think? I'm the creator of my reality anyway. I'm probably creating them to think the things I don't want them to think.

The Queen of Swords, King of Cups and **Ace of Pentacles** are now coming up in the spread. **The Queen of Swords** deals with the inner world - how you deal with conflict. She's kind of defensive, but she's not going to let you know it. You might be defensive, but you don't want anyone to know it. The reason why you're defensive, **The King of Cups** says, is because you might project your unprocessed emotions, exposing more of your true feelings than you're comfortable with.

The Ace of Pentacles says, money will be coming. **The King of Cups** is also saying, project into life what you want. Create a vision board, a treasure map, a vision for your thoughts. The **Four of Pentacles** is telling you you're holding onto old stuff that's not serving you. You want that security, so you're protecting yourself by keeping yourself locked up inside, so nobody will know what you're feeling and nobody will see your true personality. They'll see your art but they won't see you. **The Page of Wands** is showing you new thought possibilities, and the **Seven of Pentacles** has you contemplating where you are currently investing your thoughts and actions vs. where you would like them to be in the near future.

****

Merlin then says, "Yes, I am really frightened. I then tell him, "Of course you are. There's a thread of similarity in all of us. We all want the same thing. The reason for being scared is because it's scary to be "Big", to be our true Higher Self. It's so much easier to be our lower self. Being "Big" means changing our whole perception of our world and ourself. It means taking a leap of faith of getting fear out of the way and being who we truly are. We are Gods! (Gods In Training - G.I.T.s)".

Now we're on the pyramid going back down again.

<u>The Pyramid - Going Down</u>

Now we've got **The Chariot.** Oops! I've put out seven cards instead of six, so I guess he wants to be here. **The Chariot** is saying Merlin, take hold of the reins of your emotions and stay spiritually centered over the positive and negative thoughts. Looking at the stars on the roof of the chariot, this card is also telling you, your astrology can help ground you.

The **Four of Swords**, is saying to use prayer and meditation to raise your vibration and connect with spirit. The **Eight of Wands** is showing energy you are sending out to the universe. **The Wheel of Fortune** represents change. You can change the force of your luck through the meditation, prayer and spiritual centering that **The Chariot,** and the **Four of Swords** are telling you to do. Also, changing your perception with **The Hanged Man,** is exactly what you need to do, because a quick change in perception would change the entire experience of what you're going through. It could be the exact same experience, but all of a sudden you're seeing it differently.

For example: a room looks very different when the light is on, versus when the light is off. It presents a whole different viewpoint to you.

The **Three of Pentacles** is saying, that in order to get recognition coming to you, pay attention to what you're communicating with the universe about getting recognized. You need to be receptive, by allowing recognition in. The **Two of Wands** is saying to you, **envision where you want to be in the future. Don't focus on your past. Focus on the thoughts that will attract the future you want.** Imagine the world as your oyster and see the world as your game plan.

The **Temperance** card is saying, that you have to be patient and tolerant with yourself and others. The **Six of Cups** is reminding you of something from your past. The **Two of Cups** is saying, each relationship you have is a symbolic mirror of something you need to learn about yourself. What you fear about other people's responses is really just a reflection of your own projected scary feelings. You are always the creator of your own reality.

The Ace of Cups and the High Priestess next to it are saying, work on the Holy Grail of You. Tap into your Higher Self. Recognize the Divine Order in life.

With the **Justice** card, you see there is Divine Order. Be an empty vessel for The Light to enter in. Don't let all the stuff in your head from your past block out new information (messages from the Holy Spirit). Dump out the trash from the past that has been clogging your subconsciousness and allow your cup to runneth over with new inspiration, you will now have room to receive.

For so long you kept your imagined past stuck in the closet, then you shut the closet door (unconsciously) so you wouldn't have to look at that past stuff. Open that closet now and clear out the clutter of your past. Then you'll be an empty vessel again, ready to be filled up with new inspiration. Heal your relationship with yourself, with the Two of Cups, by healing your perceptions of yourself from your past. **Be patient with yourself in the process. The King of Swords is saying, you might be more than a little angry that you created all this mess, that you weren't aware was there, lurking in your subconscious. .**

The **Three of Cups** and **The Magician** are saying, "Use that magic wand of yours, Merlin, (the wand **The Magician** is holding up), to create brand new experiences, with self validation and self recognition, you can now empower yourself with, from what you've learned about yourself.

Get out, socialize with others, the **Three of Cups** is saying. Share what you've learned from your journey in life, not only in your art, but with yourself as well. Be **The Magician** they're saying, and let others experience your learned wisdom (**The Hermit**).

But then the **King of Swords**, wants to say, Merlin, you've gotten in your way before. With the **Seven of Swords**, the card of self sabotage, the old self sabotaging thoughts are not going to want to leave so easily. The ego is going to feel threatened, if he senses he's losing control of you. He wants to keep you from discovering your Higher Self. Change is scary to him. He is used to being in control.

We go back and forth with these thoughts, of positive vs. negative thinking, creating a tug of war in our head. As we learn with **The Chariot**, we need to get centered and take control of our thoughts.

The **Knight of Cups** is saying, see your life as a quest for your Holy Grail (finding your Higher Self, while in the world). Every once in a while refresh your cup, so you'll have room for new insights. With the **King of Wands,** you'll then want to project those new insights to flow through your imagination, with with the **Seven of Cups**. Then what will happen is that you're life will feel empowered, by using all your experiences, good or bad, to get insight and a fresh perspective on life.

You'll then be able to share your insights with the world, instead of fearing judgement. You will come to see that your Holy Grail is not only your consciousness, but the energy and imagination of "You", because you'll now be able to see how much you have been creating of your reality all along. Once you realize this, you can receive from the world, and also give back with the **Six of Pentacles.**

****

In conclusion, Merlin said to me, that his life has been a homage to the imagination and sees fear of succeeding had being standing in his way.

Sample Reading

1.

Begins with Celtic Block   5 minutes

2.

Pyramid Spread   (Step 1)   5 - 10 minutes

3.

Pyramid Spread (Step 2) 15 - 20 minutes

4.

Pyramid Spread (Step 3) 20 - 30 minutes

Card Keys
&
Celtic Block
Map
(Cheat Sheets)

Keywords

<u>THE MAJOR ARCANA</u>

0   **The Fool** - faith, risk, new beginnings, free spirit, Uranus

1   **The Magician** - focus, concentration , anything is possible, Mercury

2   **The High Priestess** - choice, ESP, psychic, seductress, gestation period, Moon

3   **The Empress** - abundance, creativity, mother figure, nurturing, ideal female, unconditional love, Venus

4   **The Emperor** - experience, organize, government, father figure, ideal male , Aries

5   **The Hierophant** - seeking guidance, counselor, teacher, Taurus

6   **The Lovers** - temptation, crossroads in relationships, love, partnerships, Gemini

7   **The Chariot** - drive, ambition, getting centered, car, victory, will, Cancer

8   **Strength** - courage, inner strength, chemistry, animals, compassion, Leo

9   **Hermit** - spirit guide, wisdom, meditation, solitude, Virgo

10 **Wheel Of Fortune** - change, luck, action, what goes around comes around, Jupiter

11 **Justice** - fairness, you get back what you put out into the world, Libra

12 The Hanged Man - stagnation, sacrifice, insight, change your perception, Neptune

13 Death - change, letting go, rebirth, endings and beginnings, Scorpio

14 Temperance - balance, moderation, healing, patience and tolerance, Sagittarius

15 The Devil - negative emotions, ego, materialism, Capricorn

16 The Tower - unexpected, thoughts and beliefs built on weak foundation, Mars

17 The Star - inspiration, goals, limelight, Aquarius

18 The Moon - illusions, fears of unknown, film, computers, spiritual realm, Pisces

19 The Sun - progress, rewards, let your light shine, energetic, young spirited, bliss, Sun

20 Judgement - accepting consequences, judging, transformation, Pluto

21 The World - attainment, mission accomplished, connected, pregnancy, Saturn

THE MINOR ARCANA
COURT CARDS - can represent people related to it's suit, as well as meaning of card

Pages - Messages, babies or young girl
Knights - Changes or offers, young men
Queens - Reflecting inward, women
Kings - Projecting outward, men

WANDS - Ideas and Jobs
SEASON: Spring
COURT CARDS: Fire signs - Sagittarius, Aries, Leo
Hair Color - Brown, Red, Auburn

Ace - new ideas, new projects, new jobs

Two - contemplations, options

Three - plans, ideas in action

Four - ideas established in action, security of establishment, weddings, home and family, stage

Five - confusion, inner conflicts

Six - victory over competition

Seven - self doubt, trust yourself

Eight - ideas soon to manifest, ESP

Nine - defending and standing up for your ideas

Ten - mind is overwhelmed, burdens

Page - contemplating new ideas, written messages and contracts, writing, baby, child, young girl

Knight - putting ideas into action, job changes, young man

Queen - side tracked by your emotions or subconscious, woman

King - projecting ideas for future use, man

CUPS - **Feelings, Values, Relationships**
SEASON: Summer
COURT CARDS: Water Signs - Cancer, Pisces, Scorpio
Hair Color - Blonde

Ace - new attitudes, new relationships, new feelings

Two - communication, relationships and partnerships

Three - happiness, groups, friends, parties

Four - be more conscious of your surroundings

Five - regrets over past

Six - pleasant memories of the past

Seven - imagination, confusion

Eight - soul searching

Nine - contentment, wish granted

Ten - everyone is happy, people pleasing

Page - surprises, phone messages, baby, child, young girl

Knight - proceeding slowly, possible offers, change of heart, young man

Queen - use of imagination to visualize, worry, using intuition, woman

King - projecting your vision into future, man

SWORDS - **Conflicts, Challenges**
SEASON: Fall
COURT CARDS: Air Signs - Gemini, Libra, Aquarius
Hair Color - White, Salt and Pepper

Ace - action overcoming problems

Two - not accepting reality, not ready to see something

Three - disappointment and heartbreak

Four - rest , prayer, meditation

Five - can't get along together, sour grapes, grudges, confrontation

Six - problems smoothing out, better times ahead, travel

Seven - creating problems for yourself, self sabotage, deception

Eight - temporary difficulties, limiting thoughts holding self back, fear of moving forward, phobias

Nine - tension, anxiety, feeling sorry for yourself, headaches, stressed out

Ten - problems ending, exhaustion, back and chakra issues, broken spirit

Page - defensiveness, protectiveness of self and others, baby, child, young girl

Knight - slow down, going too fast, impulsiveness, aggressiveness, young man

Queen - defensive thinking, controlling nature, insensitive, intellectual, woman

King - stubbornness, tyrant, lack of compassion, control freak, rigid, bossy, intellectual, man

Pentacles - Money, Material Things
SEASON: Winter
COURT CARDS: Earth Signs - Capricorn, Taurus, Virgo
Hair Color - Black or Dark Brown

Ace - new material things, raise, new money, gifts

Two - balancing material aspects of life, juggling options or time

Three - recognition, interview, validation, performance

Four - hanging on, need to let go, security issues

Five - lack consciousness, abandonment issues

Six - getting or asking for help, putting out to get back, karmic justice

Seven - evaluating investments of time, money and effort

Eight - working at something or needing to

Nine - peace of mind from accomplishment, fashion

Ten - material success, transitions and expansions with success

Page - too absorbed in something, student, baby, child, young girl

Knight - surveying where you'd like to be in the future, creating a vision, young man

Queen - evaluating strengths and weaknesses, woman

King - material attainment and wealth, man

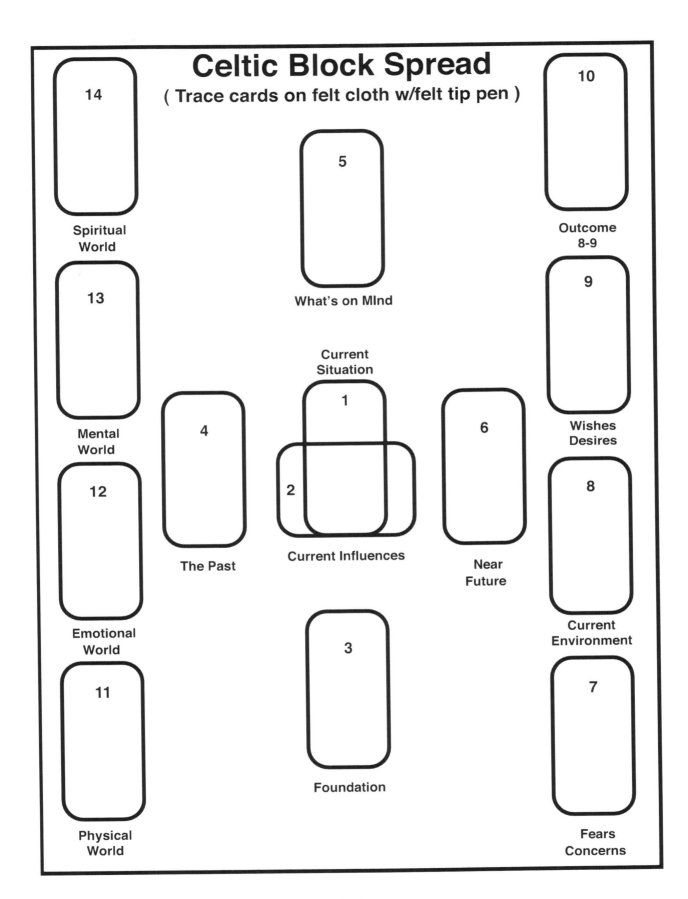

Celtic Block Spread
(Trace cards on felt cloth w/felt tip pen)

14
Spiritual
World

13
Mental
World

12
Emotional
World

11
Physical
World

5
What's on MInd

4
The Past

Current
Situation
1

2
Current Influences

3
Foundation

6
Near
Future

10
Outcome
8-9

9
Wishes
Desires

8
Current
Environment

7
Fears
Concerns

Symbols, Signs and Colors

Symbols

Archangel - Gabriel : Judgment
                    Michael : Temperance
                    Rafael : Lovers

Ankh - an ancient symbol representing life, cross of life

Bird - message from the soul, inspiration

Bull - Taurus, pentacles, earth

Butterfly - immortality, found in sword court cards

Chain - bondage or restriction

Chariot - vehicle one travels through life in, car

Crab - Cancer, emotions

Cross - union of male-female / positive -negative

Cups - values, water, emotions

Cypress tree - sorrow, mourning, sword court cards

Devil - uncontrolled desires, seeking happiness in physical pleasures, negativity, materialism, ego

Dog- man's best friend, a companion, animal nature, pet

Eagle - Scorpio, water

Earth - physical plane, manifesting

Figure eight - (sideways)lemniscate, infinity, spirit

Fish - the unexpected, cups, water

Flame - spirit

Flowers - white /spirit   red /desire

Globe - dominion, the world

Grapes - pleasure, abundance

Green healing

Hand (right)-positive / male   (left)-negative/ female

Heart - emotions

Horse - psychic energy

Ibis - ancient Egyptian bird representing inspiration

Keys - wisdom

Lamp - enlightenment

Leaves - growth

Lightning - uncontrollable force, brainstorm / enlightenment

Lion - Leo, fire, kundalini, animal nature, animals in general, inner beast

Moon - Pisces, emotions, intuition, subconscious

Mountains - (snow top) attained wisdom   (no snow) problems yet to come

Orange - emotions, energy, appetite, seeking

Pentacles - five points of human body, material world, earth

Pillar - white / positive   black / negative   link between above and below

Pomegranates - passive female energy

Purple - spirituality

Pyramid - idea, action, manifestation, material aspects of the earth

Rabbit - fertility

Rainbow - sign of happiness and protection coming from God

Rams head - Aries, fire, Mars, war, power, leadership

Red - desire, strength, here and now, sensuality

Rose - white /purity   red/ desire

Salamander - fire , wands, court cards

Scales - balance, harmony, justice

Scroll - divine law

Serpent - knowledge, wisdom (when biting tail), forever going through
     transformation,a control of subconscious to obtain wisdom

Ship - wealth

Sphinx - aspects of human and animal tendencies

Square - stability, strength, foundations

Star - (six pointed star) divine laws controlling material world
(eight pointed star) cosmic radiant energy

Stream - life force and substance of cosmic consciousness

Sunflower - fullness of nature

Swords - conflict intellect, air

Sylph - air, sword court cards

Tower - that which is made by man personality

Tree - the mind, tree of life, balance, secret of immortality

Undine - water, Queen of cups

Veil - that which is hidden

Wands - thoughts, fire

Colors

Purple - the spirit world

Indigo (midnight sky) - opening of the third eye, intuition, psychic senses

Blue (sky blue) - communication

Green - unconditional love, healing energy, fertility

Yellow - learning from the gut feelings of the solar plexus

Orange - assimilating and digesting experiences and ideas

Red - passion , sex, roots of experiences and ideas

White - pure state of being

Gray - astral realm, inner world

Black - subconscious emotions, mastery of material world, negativity

Brown - earthly matters and concerns, grounding

Secret Tips
From a Pro

Secret Tips From a Pro

1. Whether you're reading for someone else or for yourself, remember to frame your words in a positive context. Plant **positive seeds for growth, learning, encouragement and inspiration.** That is what attracts more of the same. It's what people really need and desire most.

2. Tune into the cards, your surroundings and the person being read and get a **sense of the energies present.** What are you **"feeling"**? What is your body feeling around and with the client? Feeling tense, irritated, defensive, happy, sad? **Listen to how you "feel" and trust your instincts over feedback from the client, who may not be aware of something, or not being open or receptive yet. Trust messages "you sense by energy" and don't be afraid to go with it and say it to the client.**

3. Love yourself and your clients enough to be firm with tough love about what you will and won't tolerate, so you can enjoy working together, so you will both benefit from your experiences in the readings. Trust the energy you're sensing, when something doesn't feel good to you.

4.Clear your mind before doing a reading and get your own ego out of the way. Stay positive. You want to be able to **"receive"** for the person. If your mind is full, you will have no room to receive messages.

5.Look at the pictures and the cards like you might with symbols in a dream, telling you a message to pay attention to.

6.Visualize a circle of light around you before doing a reading and ask your Spirit Guides to give you wisdom for your client. You can visualize a circle of light around the client and space you are working in as well.

The Tarot as an Interdimensional Tool: 2012 and Beyond

Humanity and Our World are about to go through a Great Shift, moving from the third dimension into the fifth dimension. Using the tarot as a tool for interdimensional communication can help prepare you for these swiftly changing times.

Much like our televisions, we, ourselves, are sending and receiving stations of vibrational frequencies. What you are "tuned into," via your point of focus and intention, will determine what channel you are on, and appear on your radar. The tarot acts as a telephone line between dimensions. By understanding and practicing it's universal language, you gradually become a "conscious" channel for receiving and transmitting messages from other dimensions. As you become comfortable working with your spirit guides, asking them for their help in translating the messages from the cards, a new world of communication will open up to you. It is then up to you to silence your logical mind to the outside noise and tune into the messages that will come from your 6th sense - information from within.

Knowing the Law of Attraction is paramount now more than ever. This universal law states that the energy from your thought based e-motion (energy in motion) attracts experiences in physical form that match up with your vibrational frequency. The tarot cards that come into your readings will mirror back to you the vibrational frequency that your current state of consciousness is attracting back to you in your world, both personally and collectively. The frequencies you send out, whether positive or negative, have a chain reaction not only in your own life, but globally and universally. We can go into this Great Shift with comfort or suffering, depending on humanity's free will choice, to go with fear based thinking or love based thinking.

Our greatest challenge right now is whether we will let love or fear based thinking rule our destiny on this beautiful planet of ours. Collectively we can choose to "Co- Create Heaven on Earth", by beginning with ourselves.

Made in the USA
Charleston, SC
22 May 2013